From the Apostles to Wesley

From the APOSTLES to WESLEY

*Christian Perfection
in Historical Perspective*

by

WILLIAM M. GREATHOUSE

BEACON HILL PRESS OF KANSAS CITY
Kansas City, Missouri

Permission to quote from the following copyrighted versions of the Bible is acknowledged with appreciation:

The *Revised Standard Version of the Bible* (RSV), copyrighted 1946, 1952, © 1971, 1973.

The Holy Bible, New International Version (NIV), copyright © 1978 by the New York International Bible Society.

Contents

Foreword

W. M. Greathouse long has occupied a place at the front rank of biblical students, historians, and interpreters of the doctrine of Christian Perfection. To his earlier excellent studies—among them *The Fullness of the Spirit* (1958)—he now has added a significant treatment of the historical expressions of the biblical teaching of full salvation.

Sharply critical of any interpretation which sees the teaching as a recent theological or "sectarian vagary," *From the Apostles to Wesley* begins with a lucid statement of the doctrine of holiness (Chapter 1) and proceeds immediately to examine its biblical basis (Chapter 2).

With a thoroughness and skill comparable to R. Newton Flew's standard work, *The Idea of Christian Perfection,* Dr. Greathouse in the remaining eight chapters traces the ways the doctrine has been interpreted and developed throughout the history of Christian thought. Each era and major Christian interpreters are noted for their distinctive contributions, and are evaluated in the light of scriptural teaching.

The author's point of view is biblically based and doctrinally sound. His critiques of each historical development are grounded in the Word of God and enlivened by an informed dialogue with the past.

Chapter 5 is particularly illuminating, especially for the place given to "Macarius the Egyptian"—whether or not his writings are those of Gregory of Nyssa, as some authorities indicate. Macarius's influence on William Law and John Wesley is demonstrated to be greater than is generally known. Showing this relationship in itself, aside from the numerous other insightful passages, is a significant contribution to holiness literature.

No one who would understand John Wesley's teaching on Christian perfection and the theological streams that flow toward him and from him can overlook this book. Numerous misinterpretations can be corrected subtly by a thoughtful read-

7

ing. Whether the reader is trained in theological exactness or is a beginner in doctrinal matters, one will read this volume with great profit.

Preachers, teachers, and laypersons alike will be better equiped to proclaim and bear witness to the glorious scriptural truth of Christian holiness.

And all who earnestly are following after holiness of heart and life and who desire increasing conformity to the mind of Christ will find that yearning intensified. Through the pen and heart of one who combines the scholarly disciplines of an educator, a warm spirit of Christlikeness, and a mature loyalty of churchmanship, one will hear the Spirit's clear call to holy living.

—JOHN A. KNIGHT, *President*
Bethany Nazarene College
Bethany, Oklahoma

Preface

What is the pedigree of the Wesleyan doctrine of Christian Perfection? Did it come fully developed from the mind of John Wesley, as Minerva sprang full-grown from the head of Jupiter, or was the teaching a fresh and creative formulation of a truth which has always lain at the heart of the Christian faith?

It is the thesis of this monograph that the teaching of Christian Perfection derives essentially from the Scriptures, and that Wesley's doctrine, far from being a sectarian vagary is, indeed, in George Croft Cell's words, "an original and unique synthesis" of the Protestant ethic of grace and the Catholic ideal of holiness.

A survey of the history of Christian thought leads to the conclusion that the doctrine of Christian Perfection—understood not as a final and absolute attainment, but as a realizable experience of heart purity and perfect love, making possible ever-increasing growth in Christlikeness—is no "theological provincialism" but the expression of a conviction which has possessed many of the greatest theologians of the Christian Church through the centuries. Joining St. Paul, St. Peter, and St. John of the New Testament Church in this faith are such greats as Irenaeus, Clement and Origen of Alexandria, Gregory of Nyssa, Augustine of Hippo, and Thomas Aquinas, "the angel doctor" of Roman Catholic theology.

While Augustine can be cited as an advocate of this truth, his pessimistic doctrine of Original Sin with its notion of ineradicable concupiscence has been the single greatest foe of the doctrine, especially in Protestantism. Developed in his controversy with Pelagius, this latter idea upstaged Augustine's earlier confidence in the possibilities of grace and became the standard view of most Reformed and Lutheran theologies. The permanent residue of Augustine's doctrine is the view that human nature is irretrievably sinful this side of the resurrection.

John Wesley was not bound by this essentially Hellenistic

9

notion of human nature and sin. Under the guidance of the Eastern church fathers especially, along with certain Roman Catholic teachers, Wesley found his way back to Holy Scripture itself, where he discovered a more Hebraic doctrine of original sin (as unbelief, pride, and self-idolatry) and recovered an apostolic confidence in the boundless power of God's grace to deliver man from sin and perfect him in love.

Colin Williams places the Wesleyan doctrine in proper perspective when he writes: "It is only in the context of the final expression of the Christian life represented in Wesley's theology that his doctrine of perfection can be understood, for perfection is the climax of the limitless faith in God's grace which shines through every part of his theology. It is here that his theology comes into focus" (*John Wesley's Theology Today*, p. 347). It is the thesis of this book that the Wesleyan doctrine represents the finest flower of Christian belief.

The standard work on this subject is R. Newton Flew's *Idea of Perfection* (Oxford University Press, 1934). Those who know this book will recognize its impress on several sections of the present volume, particularly in the treatment of Thomas Aquinas. No student of perfection can ignore Flew's *magnum opus*.

The substance of these chapters originated as talks given by the author at the National Mexican Holiness Conference in Guadalajara in February, 1978. Subsequently these lectures were enlarged to essentially their present form and translated into Spanish by Dr. Sergio Franco and published by Casa Nazarena de Publicaciones under the title *Desde de Apóstoles Hasta Wesley, Un Resumen de la perfección Cristiana*.

I owe a debt of gratitude to Dr. H. T. Reza, director of the International Publications Board of the Church of the Nazarene, who encouraged me to produce the first draft of this book and thereby put in permanent form a conviction which was born when I was a university student and which has found sporadic expression from time to time in the classroom and pulpit. I am also grateful to Mrs. Gene Van Note and Miss Mary Ann Wagner for their help in typing and preparing the manuscript for publication.

—William M. Greathouse

CHAPTER 1

The Statement of the Doctrine

John Morley, in his essay on Voltaire, remarks that holiness is the "deepest of all words that defy description."[1] Rudolph Otto later developed this thought in his classic work, *The Idea of the Holy,*[2] in which he argues that the experience of "the Holy" (the "creature-consciousness" of which St. Paul writes in Rom. 1:19-20) is the very essence of religion. To be human is to be confronted by the Holy God. For this reason, the conception of holiness, in one form or another, is as old as religion itself.

Speaking biblically, holiness has its origin in the Eternal. "Blessed be the God and Father of our Lord Jesus Christ, who has blessed us in Christ with every spiritual blessing in heavenly places, even as he chose us in him before the foundation of the

---

1. Donald S. Metz, *Studies in Biblical Holiness* (Kansas City: Beacon Hill Press of Kansas City, 1971), p. 13.
2. Rudolph Otto, *The Idea of the Holy,* trans. by John W. Harvey (London: Oxford University Press, 1924).

world, that we should be holy and blameless before him" (Eph. 1:3-4, RSV).

Holiness is the sum of *the Law's requirement*. In reply to the question, "What is the great commandment of the law?" Jesus responded by quoting Deut. 6:4-5 and Lev. 19:18: "Thou shalt love the Lord thy God with all thy heart, and with all thy soul, and with all thy mind. This is the first and great commandment. And the second is like unto it, Thou shalt love thy neighbour as thyself. On these two commandments hang all the law and the prophets" (Matt. 23:36-40).

Holiness is also *the promise of the gospel*. Strangely enough, it is in the Old Testament that we find this promise: "The Lord thy God will circumcise thine heart, and the heart of thy seed, to love the Lord thy God with all thine heart, and with all thy soul, that thou mayest live" (Deut. 30:6). John Wesley chose this idea as the theme of his first sermon on Christian perfection at Oxford University. Wesley himself describes the occasion:

> On January 1, 1733, I preached before the university in St. Mary's Church, on "The Circumcision of the Heart;" an account of which I gave in these words: "It is that habitual disposition of soul which, in the sacred writings, is termed holiness; and which directly implies the being cleansed from sin, 'from all filthiness of both flesh and spirit;' and, by consequence, the being endued with those virtues which were in Christ Jesus; the being so 'renewed in the image of the mind,' as to be 'perfect as our Father in heaven is perfect.'"
>
> In the same sermon I observed, "'Love is the fulfilling of the law, the end of the commandment.' It is not only 'the first and great' command, but all the commandments in one. 'Whatsoever things are just, whatsoever things are pure, if there be any virtue, if there be any praise,' they are all comprised in this one word, love. In this is perfection, and glory, and happiness. The royal law of heaven and earth is this, 'Thou shalt love the Lord thy God with all thy heart, and with all thy soul, and with all thy mind, and with all thy strength.'"[3]

The doctrine of Christian Perfection, or Christian Holiness, is the glorious teaching that through the provisions of the Sacrifice of Christ and the personal agency of the Holy Spirit, and on the condition of simple faith, those who savingly trust in Christ

---

3. "A Plain Account of Christian Perfection," *The Works of John Wesley* (Kansas City: Nazarene Publishing House, n.d.), 11:367-68.

may be cleansed from original sin, or depravity, and brought into a state of entire devotement to God and unselfish love for their fellowman.

This, we believe, is what it means to be "perfect" in the scriptural sense. "The word [perfect] has various senses," Wesley explains; "here it means perfect love. It is love excluding sin; love filling the heart, taking up the whole capacity of the soul."[4]

A. Sanctification

The word *sanctification*, like the kindred term *holiness*, has various meanings which it is important to note.[5]

1. *Sanctification in General*

In general terms, *sanctification* refers to the total process of becoming and remaining a Christian. As Lueker explains, "In its wider sense, the term *sanctification* includes all those effects of God's word produced on the heart and life of man, beginning with his rebirth from spiritual death to spiritual life and culminating in spiritual perfection in life eternal."[6] Another writer asserts, "Sanctification is the work of the Holy Spirit of God, in delivering men from the guilt and power of sin, in consecrating them to the service and love of God, and imparting to them, initially and progressively, the fruits of Christ's redemption and the graces of the holy life."[7]

2. *Positional Sanctification*

Lutheran and Calvinistic theologians have generally espoused the idea of positional sanctification or holiness. A contemporary interpreter of Luther writes:

> Because faith receives and accepts the gift of God and thus men become saints through faith, "holy" becomes the equivalent of "believing." The saints, or holy ones, are the believers and "to make holy" means "to be made a believer." In Luther's explanation the emphasis is shifted from sanctify

---

4. "The Scripture Way of Salvation," *Works*, 6:46.

5. In this section the writer is dependent on the excellent treatment of the subject by Metz, *Studies in Biblical Holiness*, pp. 15-20.

6. E. L. Lueker, ed., *Lutheran Cyclopedia* (St. Louis: Concordia Publishing House, 1954), p. 942.

7. *Encyclopedia of Religion and Ethics*, ed. James Hastings (New York: Charles Scribner's Sons, 1928), 11:181.

and sanctifying to faith and being brought to faith except that there is no real difference between the two.[8]

John F. Walvoord explains that "positional perfection is revealed to be the possession of every Christian. . . . It is, therefore, absolute perfection, which Christ wrought for us on the cross. There is no reference here to the quality of the Christian life. The issue of sinlessness is not in view. All saints (sanctified ones) are partakers of the perfection accomplished by the death of Christ." Positional perfection is a synonym for positional sanctification, which is "wrought by Christ for every believer, and which is the possession of the believer from the moment of saving faith."[9]

Wesleyans accept this view, since it is an aspect of scriptural teaching. Sanctification, says Turner, is "the ascription of sanctity to persons by virtue of their relationship to God. It is in this lowest sense that all Christians are said to be holy, or to be saints. The Christian Church is regarded as a separated community, the nature of which is to be holy."[10]

From the Wesleyan point of view, however, sanctification is more than an objective relationship to God through Christ. At the moment this new relationship is established through faith in Christ, the justified believer receives the Holy Spirit and experiences the beginnings of ethical sanctification. This beginning of spiritual life we term initial sanctification.

3. Initial Sanctification

In replying to a question regarding the time sanctification begins, Wesley replied, "In the moment we are justified, the seed of every virtue is then sown in the soul. From that time the believer gradually dies to sin, and grows in grace. Yet sin remains in him; yea, the seed of all sin till he is sanctified throughout in spirit, soul, and body."[11] For Wesley, sanctification in this initial sense is the ethical counterpart of justification. "At the same time that we are justified," he explains, "yea, in that

---

8. Herbert Girgensohn, *Teaching Luther's Catechism,* trans. John W. Doberstein (Philadelphia: Muhlenberg Press, 1959), p. 180.

9. John F. Walvoord, *Doctrine of the Holy Spirit* (3rd ed.: Findlay, Ohio: Dunham Publishing Co., 1958), pp. 208, 210.

10. George Allen Turner, *The More Excellent Way* (Winona Lake, Ind.: Light and Life Press, 1952), p. 87.

11. *Works,* 8:285

very moment, sanctification begins. In that instant we are born again, born from above, born of the Spirit: there is a *real* as well as a *relative* change. We are inwardly renewed by the power of God."[12] Initial sanctification is therefore practically synonymous with regeneration. To be made alive to God through the Spirit is to be set on the path to perfection.

4. *Progressive Sanctification*

With most Protestant thinkers, Wesleyans teach progressive sanctification defined in the Westminster Catechism as "the work of God's free grace, whereby we are renewed in the whole man after the image of God, and are enabled more and more to die unto sin and live unto righteousness."[13] Abraham Kuyper writes:

> Mere regeneration does not sanctify his inclination and disposition; nor is it able of itself to germinate the holy disposition. But it requires the Holy Spirit's *additional* and very *peculiar* act, whereby the *disposition* of the regenerated and converted sinner is brought gradually into harmony with the divine will; and this is the gracious gift of sanctification.[14]

The distinctive teaching of John Wesley is that this work of interior sanctification may be cut short in a "moment," by faith, when the heart is cleansed from the inward root of sin—pride, self-will, atheism, or idolatry—and perfected in the love of God. As a consequence of this deeper cleansing of the heart the Christian is enabled to grow more normally toward perfected Christlikeness. Article X of the *Manual* of the Church of the Nazarene states:

> We believe that the grace of entire sanctification includes the impulse to grow in grace. However, this impulse must be continuously nurtured, and careful attention given to the requisites and processes of spiritual development and improvement in Christlikeness of character and personality. Without such purposeful endeavor one's witness may be impaired and the grace itself frustrated and ultimately lost.

5. *Entire Sanctification*

In his sermon "Working Out Our Own Salvation," John

---

12. *Works*, 6:45.

13. *The Assembly's Shorter Catechism* (Perth, Scotland: 1765), p. 222.

14. Abraham Kuyper, *The Work of the Holy Spirit*, trans. by Henri DeVries (New York: Funk and Wagnalls, 1900), p. 449.

Wesley places the grace of entire sanctification in its proper context:

> By justification we are saved from guilt of sin, and restored to the favour of God; by sanctification, we are saved from the power and root of sin, and restored to the image of God. All experience, as well as Scripture, show this salvation to be both instantaneous and gradual. It begins the moment we are justified, in the holy, humble, gentle, patient love of God and man. It gradually increases from that moment . . . *till, in another instant, the heart is cleansed from all sin, and filled with pure love to God and man.* But even that love increases more and more, till we "grow up in all things into Him that is our Head;" till we attain "the measure of the stature of the fulness of Christ."[15]

In addition to the above terms there is one additional term which requires explanation, namely, Perfection or Christian Perfection.

6. *Perfection*

This term has been the cause of criticism to the holiness movement, but it is a biblical word and a term which has been associated with the teaching of holiness throughout the Christian centuries. As far as Wesley is concerned, he used the term because it "is *scriptural,* and Wesley was passionately attached to the language of Scripture."[16] He summarized his teachings on holiness in a small book he entitled *A Plain Account of Christian Perfection.* Metz correctly observes: "Wesley's definition of perfection is as yet unimproved and still carries the essence of what is meant by the term in holiness circles. Wesley preferred to use *Christian perfection* rather than the more unqualified term *perfection.*"[17] At the end of the *Plain Account,* Wesley sums up his teaching in these words: "By perfection I mean the humble, gentle, patient love of God, and our neighbour, ruling our tempers, words, and actions."[18] He was careful to guard against a Pharisaic or legalistic view of perfection, insisting at all times that "there is no such perfection in this life, as implies

---

15. *Works,* 6:509 (italics added).
16. W. E. Sangster, *The Path to Perfection* (New York: Abingdon-Cokesbury Press, 1943), p. 78.
17. Metz, *Studies in Biblical Holiness,* p. 20.
18. *Works,* 11:446.

an entire deliverance, either from ignorance, or mistake, in things not essential to salvation, or from manifold temptations, or from numberless infirmities, wherewith the corruptible body more or less presses down the soul."[19]

For Wesley, as for Scripture, Christian Perfection means *perfect love*. This is the sense in which it has been understood by the clearest exponents of the teaching through the centuries, as we shall see in the course of this book. In his sermon on Christian Perfection, Wesley therefore says, "It is only another term for holiness. They are two names for the same thing."[20]

19. *Ibid.*, p. 383.
20. *Works*, 6:6.

CHAPTER 2

The Biblical Doctrine

The original and the only authoritative source of the teaching of Christian holiness is the written Word of God. It is not without reason that the Scriptures are called "the Holy Bible." The Bible is a book of holiness.

The classic word on this matter was spoken by Bishop Foster:

> Holiness breathes in the prophecy, thunders in the law, murmurs in the narrative, whispers in the promises, supplicates in the prayers, sparkles in the poetry, resounds in the songs, speaks in the types, glows in the imagery, voices in the language, and burns in the spirit of the whole scheme, from alpha to omega, from its beginning to its end. Holiness! holiness needed! holiness required! holiness offered! holiness attainable! holiness a present duty, a present privilege, a present enjoyment, is the progress and completeness of its wondrous theme! It is the truth glowing all over, webbing all through revelation; the glorious truth which sparkles and whispers, and sings and shouts in all its history, and biography, and poetry, and prophecy, and precept, and promise,

and prayer; the great central truth of the system. The wonder is that all do not see, that any rise up to question, a truth so conspicuous, so glorious, so full of comfort.[1]

A. Old Testament Roots of the Doctrine

With the recent upsurge of biblical theology a number of excellent studies of Old Testament theology have appeared. As a consequence, our understanding of the Old Testament teaching of holiness has been greatly enriched. This is true particularly with respect to the revelation of the holiness of God in the pre-Christian Scriptures.

1. *The Holiness of God*

Biblical theology has demonstrated conclusively that holiness is not merely one of God's attributes or even the chief moral attribute. Typical of the best biblical scholarship is the position of Jacob, who writes, "Holiness is not one divine quality among others, even the chiefest, for it expresses what is characteristic of God and corresponds precisely to his deity."[2] Supportive of this statement is an observation by Snaith:

> When the prophet says in Amos 4:2 that Jehovah "hath sworn by his holiness," he means that Jehovah has sworn by His Deity, by Himself as God, and the meaning is therefore exactly the same as Amos 6:8, where Amos says that "the Lord God hath sworn by Himself."[3]

A student of Rabbinic literature observes that the most frequent name for God among the rabbis is "the Holy One."[4] This reflects the prophetic name of God, "the Holy One of Israel."[5] Aulén states that

> holiness is the foundation on which the whole conception of God rests. . . . In addition, it gives specific tone to each of the various elements in the idea of God and makes them part of a fuller conception of *God.* Every statement about God, wheth-

---

1. Quoted by H. Orton Wiley and Paul Culbertson, *Introduction to Christian Theology* (Kansas City: Beacon Hill Press, 1945), p. 297.

2. Edmond Jacob, *Theology of the Old Testament,* trans. by Arthur W. Heathcoat and Philip J. Allcock (New York: Harper and Brothers, 1958), p. 86.

3. Norman H. Snaith, *The Distinctive Ideas of the Old Testament* (London: The Epworth Press, 1960), p. 43.

4. Solomon Schechter, *Some Aspects of Rabbinic Theology* (New York: The Macmillan Co., 1910), p. 199.

5. Isaiah uses the term at least 30 times.

er in reference to his love, power, righteousness . . . ceases to be affirmation about God when it is not projected against the background of his holiness.[6]

The Hebrew word for holiness is *qodesh,* which, with its cognates, appears more than 830 times in the Old Testament. Scholars find three fundamental meanings in *qodesh.* (1) Often it carries the idea of "breaking forth with splendor." "There is no clear distinction between holiness and glory."[7] (2) The word also expresses a cut, a separation, an elevation. (3) *Qodesh* probably came from two roots, one of which means "new," "fresh," "pure." Holiness means purity, whether ceremonial or moral. Cleanness and holiness are virtually synonymous ideas.

As God, He shines forth with a *glory* peculiar to himself. He was manifest in the burning bush, the pillar of fire, and on flaming Sinai. Of the tabernacle the Lord said, "It shall be sanctified by my glory" (Exod. 29:43). "I will be sanctified in them that come nigh me, and before all the people I will be glorified" (Lev. 10:3). In the lofty vision of Isaiah the account reads, "Holy, holy, holy, is the Lord of hosts; the whole earth is full of his glory" (Isa. 6:3).

As God, He is *separate* from all creation. Holiness is the very nature of the divine, that which characterizes God as God and evokes worship from man. God is the "Wholly Other," standing apart from other, imaginary gods. "There is none holy as the Lord: for there is none beside thee" (1 Sam. 2:2). God's holiness means His differentness, His uniqueness as Creator, Lord, and Redeemer. Brunner says, "Only He who says, 'I, even I, am the Lord, and beside Me there is no Saviour'—can be 'the Holy One of Israel.'"[8] Yet His transcendence and separateness do not mean remoteness. As Snaith observes, "God was from the beginning transcendent in that He was different from man, but He was by no means transcendent in that He was remote from man. *I am God, and not man: the Holy One in the midst of thee,* Hosea xi 9. . . . Transcendence does not mean remoteness. It means otherness."[9]

---

6. Gustaf Aulén, *The Faith of the Christian Church,* trans. by Eric H. Wahlstrom (Philadelphia: Fortress Press, 1960), p. 132.

7. Jacob, *Theology of the Old Testament,* p. 88.

8. Emil Brunner, trans. by Olive Wyon, *The Christian Doctrine of God* (London: Lutterworth Press, 1960), p. 159.

9. Snaith, *Distinctive Ideas of the Old Testament,* p. 47.

As God, He is *sublime purity*. It is impossible for the Holy One to tolerate sin. In Genesis He is concerned with the evil imagination which pervaded mankind (Gen. 6:1-6). God's holiness is perturbed by the chronic perversity of man's heart (Jer. 3:17, 21; 17:9-10). He is of purer eyes than to behold iniquity (Hab. 1:13). When the prophet glimpsed God's holiness he cried out, "Woe is me! for I am undone; because I am a man of unclean lips, and I dwell in the midst of a people of unclean lips" (Isa. 6:5). Later Isaiah exclaims, "Who among us can dwell with the devouring fire? Who among us can dwell with the everlasting burnings?" (Isa. 33:14, RSV). God's holiness is a devouring fire which will either purge away our sin or destroy us with it! As Jesus warned, "Every one shall be salted with fire" (Mark 9:49) —either the refining fire which makes us holy (Mal. 3:2-3) or the wrath which destroys us (Mal. 4:1).

2. Sanctification

"Ye shall be holy, for I the Lord your God am holy" (Lev. 19:2). This command refers to both morals and ritual, as a reading of the holiness code (Leviticus 17—26) shows. In the earliest days of Israel's history the ritual or cultic elements of holiness were paramount, but the ethical was also present. In the prophets, the moral and ethical concerns of holiness were predominant, but the ritual was never completely lost. C. Ryder Smith thus says, "While the doctrine of the holiness of Israel described at first a distictive way-of-life in which ritual and ethics were blent indistinguishably, at the last it denoted a way-of-life where the two were still blent but in which ethics were the essential and paramount element."[10] Edersheim writes in the same vein:

> The Hebrew term for "Holy" is generally supposed to mean "separated, set apart." But this is only its secondary signification, derived from the purpose of that which is holy. Its primary meaning is to be splendid, beautiful, pure, and uncontaminated. God is holy—as the Absolutely Pure, Resplendent, and Glorious One. Hence this is symbolized by the light. God dwelleth in light that is unapproachable. . . . And Israel was to be a holy people as dwelling in the light, through its covenant-relationship to God.

---

10. C. Ryder Smith, *The Bible Doctrine of Man* (London: The Epworth Press, 1951), p. 46.

It was not the selection of Israel from all other nations that made them holy, but the relationship to God into which it brought the people. The call of Israel, their election and selection, were only the means. Holiness itself was to be attained through the covenant, which provided forgiveness and sanctification, and in which by the discipline of His law and the guidance of His Holy Arm, Israel was to be led onward and upward. Thus, if God showed the excellence of His name in creation, the way of His holiness was among Israel.[11]

Bowman distinguishes the priestly and the prophetic meanings of holiness. The priestly idea is that of being set apart, dedicated, separate. The "holy" is that which has been *separated to God*. In this sense the Temple, the priesthood, the tithe, the Sabbath, the entire nation were "holy." The prophetic idea is ethical as in Isaiah 6 and Malachi 3. Both meanings, as we have seen, combine in the "holiness code" of Leviticus 19, where a sublime ethical passage climaxes, "Thou shalt love thy neighbour as thyself: I am the Lord" (see vv. 9-18). "The New Testament, finally, takes up only the prophetic side of the term and perpetuates it. All Christians are to be 'saints' (holy ones— Rom. 1:7), that is, ethically holy, separated, consecrated to God's service (Mark 6:20; John 17:17; Rev. 3:7), that they may have fellowship with the holy God (Acts 9:13; Rom. 1:7; Heb. 6:10; Rev. 5:8)."[12]

Walther Eichrodt makes the same point:

The decisive element in the concept of holiness is shown to be that of belonging to God. . . . [But] the man who belongs to God must possess a particular kind of nature, which by comprising at once outward and inward, ritual and moral purity, will correspond to the nature of the holy God.[13]

The vision of Isaiah in the Temple clearly reveals the ethical nature of holiness as it relates to human experience. God's holiness communicates itself to the worshiper and becomes a sanctifying fire which purges the inner nature. The result of this purging of Isaiah's heart was the affirmation and enlargement of his prophetic mission. "The Lord of hosts is exalted in

11. Alfred Edersheim, *Bible History: Old Testament* (Grand Rapids: William B. Eerdmans Publishing Co., 1949 reprint), 2:110.

12. John Wick Bowman, *Prophetic Realism and the Gospel* (Philadelphia: Westminster Press, 1955), pp. 161-63.

13. Walther Eichrodt, *Theology of the Old Testament*, trans. by J. A. Baker (Philadelphia: Westminster Press, 1961), 1:137.

justice, and the Holy God shows himself holy in righteousness"
(Isa. 5:16, RSV).

3. Perfection

In the preaching of the prophets God's holiness becomes a demand for personal righteousness and social justice. It is in this blending of holiness and righteousness that God's call to perfection may be understood. Turner observes,

> Of God it is said, "His way is perfect" (Ps. 18:30); but the God-fearing man also should, indeed must, "walk" with God in this "perfect way" (Ps. 18:32; 101:2, 6). A revelation of God involves a recognition of His unique holiness. This in turn discloses man's lack of holiness, his sinfulness, his need of mercy. *Sanctification is God's gracious act in the removal of sin and conformity of obedient men to God's perfection in righteousness. The consequence of this sequence is man's perfection in righteousness.*[14]

The Hebrew terms for perfection signify wholeness, righteousness, uprightness, blamelessness, perfect peace. One way of expressing the idea in the Old Testament was the metaphorical expression of "walking with God" in fidelity and fellowship. Enoch "walked with God" (Gen. 5:22, 24). In Heb. 11:5 the translation renders it "pleased God." Of Noah it is said also that he "walked with God" (Gen. 6:9), in contrast to his neighbors. Abraham was also commanded, "Walk before me, and be thou perfect" (Gen. 17:1).

In addition to being great poetry concerning the problem of unjust suffering, the Book of Job is a treatise on perfection. In this book Job is presented as "pious and upright" (literally, perfect and straight), "God-fearing and removed from evil" (Job 1:1). This claim, which is admitted with reservations by Satan, is denied by Job's "friends." While the problem of evil is left unanswered, Job's position is vindicated. In the prologue Satan admits Job's righteousness but is cynical as to his motive, insisting that Job's uprightness is selfishly motivated by a desire for gain. Remove these conditions, he challenges, and Job will rebel. Job stands the test and thereby proves the Lord's claim that his righteousness is sincere and therefore genuine. Job's perfection was a matter of *motive,* of his *disinterested love* of

---

14. George Allen Turner, *The Vision Which Transforms* (Kansas City: Beacon Hill Press, 1964), p. 41.

God. Job's heart was perfect before God because his intention was pure. This is the basic Old Testament idea of perfection.

With the exception of the Decalogue, probably no other Old Testament passage influenced the Jewish people so much as the *Shema*, which has been called the creed of Israel: "Hear, O Israel: The Lord our God is one Lord: And thou shalt love the Lord thy God with all thine heart, and with all thy soul, and with all thy might" (Deut. 6:4-5). Love is said to be the motive of the Lord's choice of Israel, and love proven by obedience, the proper response (Deut. 7:6-11).

To make possible this perfection in love there must be an excision of inner perversity. However, there is provision for drastic surgery to bring this about: "The Lord thy God will circumcise thine heart, and the heart of thy seed, to love the Lord thy God with all thine heart, and with all thy soul, that thou mayest live" (Deut. 30:6). This becomes the great New Testament doctrine of heart-circumcision by the Holy Spirit (Rom. 2:29; Col. 2:12). By the circumcision of the heart and the removal of inward sin, perfect love is made possible for the people of God! This is John Wesley's doctrine of Christian Perfection (see c. 1).

B. The New Testament Doctrine

1. *The Promise of Pentecost*

Could men be holy before the time of Christ? Isaiah's Temple experience is a glowing affirmative answer. Perfection was possible under the Old Covenant. But it was only the spiritually elite who were given the privilege of a sanctifying vision of the Lord; the rank and file were locked up under the Law and remained in the valley of repeated failure (Heb. 10:1-4; cf. Rom. 7:7-25). Before all could know freedom from sin and perfection of love, a spiritual outpouring upon the people of God must intervene. It was this effusion of the Spirit of God to which the prophets looked forward with yearning anticipation.

Through Jeremiah God says concerning that new day: "I will put my law in their inward parts, and write it in their hearts; and will be their God, and they shall be my people. And they shall teach no more every man his neighbour, and every man his brother, saying, Know the Lord: for they shall all know me, from the least of them unto the greatest" (Jer. 31:33-34).

Ezekiel also voices the same prophecy: "Then will I sprinkle clean water upon you, and ye shall be clean: . . . A new heart also will I give you, a new spirit will I put within you: . . . And I will put my spirit within you, and cause you to walk in my statutes" (Ezek. 36:25-27).

In the mouth of Joel the Lord says concerning that day: "I will pour out my spirit upon all flesh" (Joel 2:27-29). It is significant that the Jewish rabbis interpreted these and similar promises as descriptive of a future sanctifying activity of the Spirit of God which would characterize the Messianic age. Typical of rabbinic literature is the paraphrase of Ezekiel by S. Simeon b. Johai: "And God said, 'In this age, because the evil impulse exists in you, ye have sinned against me; but in the age to come I will eradicate it from you.'"[15]

The key New Testament holiness text is the declaration of Simon Peter on the Day of Pentecost, "This is that which was spoken by the prophet Joel" (Acts 2:16 ff.). The long-expected outpouring of the Spirit had come. The Spirit era which Ezekiel foresaw was here. Jeremiah's prophecy had become history, as the writer to the Hebrews says, "For by a single offering he has perfected for all time those who are sanctified. And the Holy Spirit also bears witness to us; for after saying, 'This is the covenant that I will make with them after those days, says the Lord: I will put my laws on their hearts, and write them on their minds,' then he adds, 'I will remember their sins and their misdeeds no more'" (Heb. 10:14-17, RSV).

The importance of this truth can scarcely be overemphasized. Rather than being peripheral, sanctification is at the very heart of the New Covenant. Heralding the Messiah's coming and echoing Malachi, John the Bapist said, "I baptize you with water for repentance, but . . . he will baptize you with the Holy Spirit and fire" (Matt. 3:11-12, RSV).

Miller observes:

> This . . . is the constant emphasis of the New Testament —the work, the presence, the purity, the power of the Holy Spirit. Dispensationally all was to climax in Him. His coming to the individual heart of the believer in purifying, empowering presence was the final fruition of the ages.[16]

---

15. Turner, *More Excellent Way*, p. 57.

16. Howard V. Miller, *When He Is Come* (Kansas City: Beacon Hill Press, 1941), p. 10.

John Wesley saw this clearly and made the point in his *A Plain Account of Christian Perfection:*

> The privileges of Christians are in nowise to be measured by what the Old Testament records concerning those who were under the Jewish dispensation, seeing the fulness of time is now come, the Holy Ghost is now given, *the great salvation* is now brought to men by the revelation of Jesus Christ.[17]

2. *The Meaning of Sanctification*

The New Testament doctrine is built solidly upon the foundation of the Old Testament teaching. A careful survey of New Testament references to the subject indicates that while the prophetic-ethical teaching is dominant, the cultic-religious meaning is retained.

The Christian Church is said to be a "holy nation," in which all the people constitute a "holy priesthood" (1 Pet. 2:9-10). From another perspective it is a "holy temple" (1 Cor. 3:17; Eph. 2:21; cf. 1 Pet. 2:5). For this reason all Christians are saints, or "holy ones." This title is found 61 times. But even more emphatically than in the Old Testament, cultic holiness demands ethical purity: "As he who called you is holy, be holy yourselves in all your conduct" (1 Pet. 1:15, RSV). Implicit sanctification must become explicit by the all-pervasive hallowing of life.

The central idea of Christianity is the purification of the heart from sin and its renewal in the image of God. Under *hagiazo* (the Greek verb meaning to sanctify) Thayer lists two kinds of purification: (1) "to purify by expiation, free from guilt of sin"; (2) "to purify internally by reformation of soul." This corresponds to the two epochs we call justification (with the new birth) and entire sanctification.

In justification and regeneration there is "purification by expiation of the guilt of sin" (1 Cor. 6:11; Jas. 4:8*a*). Wiley refers to this as the cleansing from *acquired* depravity.[18] By the "washing of regeneration" (Tit. 3:5) the pollution acquired by our sinning is removed and we are made "clean" (John 15:3). For this reason sanctification is said to begin in regeneration.

---

17. *Works,* 11:375.

18. H. Orton Wiley, *Christian Theology* (Kansas City: Beacon Hill Press, 1945), 2:480.

Negatively, entire sanctification purifies the heart from the root or inbeing of sin, effecting single-mindedness of devotion to God (John 17:17, 19; Eph. 5:26; 1 Thess. 5:23; James 4:8b). Entire sanctification is not so much a state as a condition preserved moment by moment as we walk in the light (1 John 1:7).

Positively, sanctification is the restoration of the moral image of God "in true righteousness and holiness" (Eph. 4:24, RSV). This positive sanctification includes a progressive work. It is initiated in regeneration, accelerated by the cleansing of the heart and the infilling of the Spirit, and consummated by glorification. The process is beautifully depicted by Paul in these words: "We all, with unveiled face, beholding the glory of the Lord, are being changed into his likeness from one degree of glory to another" (2 Cor. 3:18, RSV).

a. Sanctification as total process. The word *hagiasmos* occurs 10 times in the New Testament and is rendered "sanctification" in each instance by the American Revised and New American Standard versions. The word "connotes state and that not native to its subject but as an outcome of action or progress."[19] The broad meaning of *hagiasmos,* signifying the total process of sanctification, is indicated in 1 Cor. 1:30; 2 Thess. 2:13; and Heb. 12:14.

Viewed ethically, salvation *is* sanctification—the hallowing of our lives by the sanctifying Spirit. From beginning to end our personal sanctification is His gracious work *in* us. This sanctification is all of a piece, a "continuity of grace" carried forward by the Holy Spirit. "The Holy Spirit," says John Wesley, "is not only holy in himself, but the immediate cause of all holiness in us."

b. Initial sanctification. Sanctification begins in regeneration. The new life principle imparted by the Holy Spirit is a principle of holiness. "The love of God is shed abroad in our hearts by the Holy Ghost which is given unto us" (Rom. 5:5). Writing to the Corinthian church Paul said, "Know ye not that the unrighteous shall not inherit the kingdom of God? Be not deceived: Neither fornicators, nor idolaters, nor adulterers . . . shall inherit the kingdom of God. And such were some of you: but ye are *washed,* but ye are *sanctified,* but ye are *justified* in the name of the Lord Jesus, and by the Spirit of our God" (1 Cor.

---

19. Turner, *More Excellent Way,* p. 83.

6:9-11, italics added). In his sermon "Sin in Believers," Wesley comments on this passage:

> "Ye are washed," says the apostle, "ye are sanctified;" namely, cleansed from "fornication, idolatry, drunkenness," and all other *outward* sin; and yet, at the same time, in another sense of the word, they were unsanctified; they were not washed, not *inwardly* cleansed from envy, evil surmising, partiality.[20]

We therefore speak of initial sanctification as partial rather than entire. This term, says Wiley, "is not an indefinite one, referring to the cleansing away of more or less of the sinner's defilement. It is a definite term, and is limited strictly to that guilt and acquired depravity attaching to actual sins, for which the sinner is himself responsible."[21]

Initial or partial sanctification is also implied by Paul's exhortation in 2 Cor. 7:1, where he urges his readers, "Having therefore these promises, dearly beloved, let us cleanse ourselves from all filthiness of the flesh and spirit, *perfecting holiness* in the fear of God." This verse argues for both initial and entire sanctification. The Corinthians were to bring to completion a holiness which was only partial.

c. Entire sanctification. Although implied by many New Testament passages, the doctrine of entire sanctification seems to be *demanded* by others, including John 17:17, 19; Rom. 6:12-13; 12:1-2; 2 Cor. 7:1; Eph. 1:4; 5:26; 1 Thess. 5:23; Tit. 2:14; and perhaps Heb. 13:12. It would take us beyond the scope of this book to exegete all these passages, but a few comments may be in order.

In Romans 6 Paul exhorts the Roman Christians, in view of their conversion and baptism, to: (1) consider themselves dead to sin and alive to God in Christ Jesus (6:11); (2) desist from putting the members of their bodies at the disposal of sin (6:12); and (3) yield or present themselves to God "as men who have been brought from death to life" (6:13, RSV). The relation of this act of yielding faith to true sanctification is indicated in verse 19: "Just as you once yielded your members to impurity and to greater and greater iniquity, so now yield your members to righteousness *for sanctification*" (RSV). Romans 12:1-2

---

20. *Works,* 5:150.
21. Wiley, *Christian Theology,* 2:480.

repeats the same exhortation to consecration for complete holiness.

Ephesians 5:25-27 moves in the same vein: "Christ loved the church and gave himself up for her, that he might sanctify her, *having cleansed her* by the washing of water with the word, that the church might be presented before him in splendor, without spot or wrinkle or any such thing, that she might be holy and without blemish" (RSV). Christ gave himself up to sanctify the Church *which has already had the bath of regeneration.* Verse 27 informs us that this sanctification accomplishes the blamelessness set forth in 1:4.

In 1 Thessalonians, Paul rejoices that his converts received the gospel "in power, and in the Holy Ghost, and in much assurance" (1:5); but his prayer is that their faith might be perfected (3:10), "to the end he may stablish your hearts unblameable in holiness before God, even our Father, at the coming of our Lord Jesus Christ" (3:13). He goes on to remind his readers that this sanctification is God's will and call to those to whom He had already given the Holy Spirit (4:3-8). The climax of his appeal is 5:14-24. The burden of the entire letter finds expression in verses 23-24: "The very God of peace sanctify you wholly; and I pray God your whole spirit and soul and body be preserved blameless unto the coming of our Lord Jesus Christ. Faithful is he that calleth you, who also will do it." The adverb translated "wholly" is the strongest word Paul could employ. It is a compound word meaning "entirely" and "perfectly." Commenting on this prayer, Morris writes:

> The prayer is that God may *sanctify you wholly.* There is a manward aspect of sanctification in that we are called upon to yield up our wills for the doing of God's will. But the power manifest in the sanctified life is not human, but divine, and Paul's prayer is phrased in the light of this. In the deepest sense our sanctification is the work of God within us. The work may be ascribed to the Son (Eph. v. 26) or to the Spirit (Rom. xv. 16), but in any case it is divine. The word *wholly* is an unusual one *(holoteleis),* being found only here in the New Testament. It is a combination of the ideas of wholeness and completeness, and Lightfoot suggests that the meaning may be given here as "may He sanctify you so that you may be entire."[22]

---

22. Leon Morris, *The Epistles of Paul to the Thessalonians* (Grand Rapids: William B. Eerdmans Publishing Co., 1957), p. 107.

The second part of this petition shows that Paul is uttering a prayer that *the entire man,* "intact in all its parts" may be *preserved* holy and blameless until the Parousia. "The faithfulness of God," Morris notes, "is the ground for certainty that the prayer offered will be answered."[23]

3. Christian Perfection

Christian Perfection and entire sanctification are two terms that describe the same experience of God's grace. Perfection in love before God *is* Christian holiness.

The verb *teleioō,* translated "perfect," occurs 25 times in the New Testament. It means (1) to realize an end, attain to a certain norm or standard, achieve a given purpose; and (2) to fulfill or complete. Paul uses the adjective *teleiōs* seven times. In several instances the meaning is clearly "mature" in the moral sense (1 Cor. 14:20; Eph. 4:13-14). In 1 Cor. 2:6, 15, however, the "perfect" are equated with the "spiritual" (also in 1 Cor. 3:1). A study of the latter passage indicates that the "perfect" are the fully sanctified. J. Weiss concludes that while perfection is usually future in Paul (Phil. 3:12), yet sometimes (1 Cor. 2:6; Phil. 3:15) it is already present.[24] He holds that Paul's use of *teleiōs* in Col. 1:28 and 4:12 designates moral and spiritual perfection.

The evidence, therefore, points to a double meaning of perfection. A Christian may be both perfect and imperfect, depending upon the sense in which the words are used. A *relative* perfection is now a possibility through faith and the Spirit, but *final* perfection awaits the resurrection (Phil. 3:11-12, 20-21).

a. Perfection in love. One of the most important sections on perfection is Matt. 5:43-48, climaxing with the Master's command: "You, therefore, must be perfect, as your heavenly Father is perfect" (RSV). "Therefore" is the key to this text. Jesus is saying, in effect, "As your Father is perfect in love, sending His blessings upon friend and enemy alike, you must be perfect in your love toward all men." It is evident that this is the love of *agape*—spontaneous, undefeatable good will, arising from the inner life of a person indwelt by the Spirit. As such,

---

23. *Ibid.,* p. 108.
24. Quoted by Turner, *More Excellent Way,* p. 95.

perfect love is both the *gift* (Rom. 5:5; 8:3-4; 1 John 4:13-17) and *command* of God (Mark 12:29-31; 1 John 4:21).

When this love is expressed the law is fulfilled (Matt. 22:40; 1 Tim. 1:5). "Owe no one anything, except to love one another; for he who loves his neighbor has fulfilled the law. . . . Love does no wrong to a neighbor; therefore love is the fulfilling of the law" (Rom. 13:8, 9-10, RSV). Christian perfection is perfection in love.

b. Perfected Christlikeness. The final goal of perfection is completed Christlikeness, which will be God's gift at the coming of Christ (1 John 3:2). In view of this future goal every Christian must confess with Paul, "Not that I have already attained, or am already perfected" (Phil. 3:12, Wesley's translation). "There is a difference between one that is perfect," Wesley explains, "and one that is *perfected.* The one is fitted for the race; the other, ready to receive the prize."[25]

---

25. John Wesley, *Explanatory Notes upon the New Testament* (London: The Epworth Press, 1950 edition), p. 735.

CHAPTER 3

The Early Church

It would be claiming too much to say that Christian perfection as delineated in the Scriptures and understood by Wesleyan theology has been taught and believed by the Church through the centuries. Actually, this teaching has often been condemned and maligned. Nevertheless, some form of perfectionist doctrine has been held in every age, not only by the orthodox but also by those with heretical tendencies.

Extra-biblical ideas have entered the Christian tradition from various religious and philosophical systems at work in the wider world within which the Church was witnessing and working, and each of these has resulted in a reshaping of the doctrine of holiness. Non-biblical ideas of God, man, and sin have all played their part in remolding the teaching. William Burton Pope observes that these diverse principles which have contributed to mold opinion may be very profitably studied as shedding light upon the scriptural doctrine. "Indeed," as Pope says, "their respective views on this subject may be regarded as among the most searching tests which can be applied to the various systems."[1]

Despite these vagaries of teaching, the essentials of the doctrine of Christian perfection have been preserved, although with minor differences, from the very beginning. Pope correctly claims, "The Spirit of finished holiness has never left himself without witness."[2] The passing centuries have been characterized by differences of emphasis as well as of terminology, as every student of church history knows, but in no age has the truth of holiness suffered eclipse.

A. The Apostolic Fathers

The theology of the Apostolic Fathers does not move on the same high plane as the New Testament. As McGiffert points out, "Though Paul was the greatest thinker in the early church his thought was not generally understood and his interpretation of Christianity was not widely accepted."[3] A general type of Christianity very different from Paul's came to prevail, an understanding of Christ's gospel as a new law. Fear tended to replace love as the proper attitude toward God, and faith often became simply another work performed by the Christian. To obey the law is to inherit eternal life. The Epistle of Barnabas illustrates this viewpoint: "It is well to learn the ordinances of the Lord, as many as have been written, and to walk in them. For he who does these things shall be glorified in the kingdom of God; while he who chooses the other shall perish together with his works. For this reason there is a resurrection, for this reason a recompense."[4] And according to Second Clement, "If we do the will of Christ we shall find rest; but if not nothing shall deliver us from eternal punishment, if we disregard his commandments."[5] Quotations such as these could be multiplied almost endlessly from the writings of the Fathers.

-----

1. William Burton Pope, *A Compendium of Christian Theology* (London: Published for the Wesleyan Conference Office, 1880), 3:61.

2. *Ibid.*

3. A. C. McGiffert, *A History of Christian Thought* (New York: Charles Scribner's Sons, 1949), 1:30.

4. Barnabas 21:1-2.

5. 2 Clement 6:7.

Although there was widespread failure to grasp the Christian gospel as a message of freedom through Christ, the Spirit was actively at work within the Christian community. In spite of other erroneous views, witnesses to the secret of holiness were not wanting. Salvation even in its highest reaches is not dependent upon perfection of understanding but upon obedience to the Holy Spirit. For this reason it is not difficult to discover clear words of testimony and teaching on the subject of Christian Perfection scattered among the writings of the Fathers.

Just before he was martyred, Ignatius exclaimed, "I thank Thee, Lord, that thou hast vouchsafed to honor me with a perfect love toward Thee."[6] Clement of Rome wrote, "Those who have been perfected in love, through the grace of God, attain to the place of the godly in the fellowship of those who in all ages have served the glory of God in perfectness."[7] And Polycarp, speaking of faith, hope, and love, wrote: "If any man be in these, he has fulfilled the law of righteousness, for that his love is far from sin."[8] Such words as these contain the germ of the doctrine of Christian Perfection: it is the perfection of love within the righteousness of faith. The Epistles of Ignatius speak again and again of a perfect faith, of a perfect intention, and of a perfect work of holiness.[9]

B. Irenaeus

Irenaeus, bishop of Lyons in Gaul in the latter part of the second century, was one of the few really creative thinkers in the history of the Church. McGiffert claims that he was "the most influential of all the early Fathers, not simply institutionally but theologically as well."[10] A man of rare personal piety, he was steeped in New Testament thought and displayed a true affinity to the theology of Paul. His doctrine of redemption centers in the work of Christ, and his teaching of salvation highlights the outpouring of the Holy Spirit as the means of Chris-

---

6. Cited by Wiley, *Christian Theology,* 3:449.

7. *Ibid.*

8. Cited by Pope, *Christian Theology,* 3:62.

9. *Ibid.*

10. McGiffert, *History of Christian Thought,* p. 132.

tian perfection. We may rightly classify Irenaeus as a holiness theologian.

Irenaeus was the first patristic writer to provide us with a clear and comprehensive doctrine of Atonement and Redemption. "For what purpose did Christ come down from heaven?" Irenaeus asks. Answer: "That he might destroy sin, overcome death, and give life to man."[11] By this pregnant saying we may set another;

> Man had been created by God that he might have life. If now, having lost life, and having been harmed by the serpent, he were not to return to life, but were wholly abandoned to death, then God would have been defeated, and the malice of the serpent would have overcome God's will. But since God is both invincible and magnanimous, he showed his magnanimity in correcting man, and in proving all men, as we have said; but through the Second Man he found the strong one, and spoiled his goods, and annihilated death, bringing life to man who had become subject to death.[12]

Again he urges strongly, "Our Lord . . . bound the strong one and set free the weak, and gave salvation to his handiwork by *abolishing sin.*"[13]

Irenaeus' idea is clear. As Aulén puts it, "The work of Christ is first and foremost a victory over the powers which hold mankind in bondage: sin, death, and the devil. These may be said to be in a measure personified, but in any case they are objective powers, and the victory of Christ creates a new situation, bringing their rule to an end, and setting men free from their dominion."[14]

For Irenaeus, the Incarnation is absolutely essential to redemption. "He, our Lord, . . . is the Word of God the Father made the son of man. . . . Had he not as *man* overcome man's adversary, the enemy would not have been justly overcome. Again, had it not been *God* who bestowed salvation we should not have it as a secure possession. . . . The Word of God made flesh passed through every stage of life, restoring to each age fellowship with God." Taking his cue from Paul in Rom. 8:3-4,

---

11. *Against Heresies*, III, 18. 7.

12. *Ibid.*, 23. 1.

13. *Ibid.*, sviii, 6-7 (italics added).

14. Gustaf Aulén, trans. by A. G. Hebert, *Christus Victor* (New York: The Macmillan Company, 1945), p. 20.

Irenaeus continues: "The Law, being spiritual, merely displayed sin for what it is; it did not destroy it, for sin did not hold sway over spirit but over man. For he who was to destroy sin and redeem man from guilt had to enter into the very condition of man."[15]

There is no trace of cleavage in Irenaeus between Incarnation and Atonement, which appears in Anselm and later Satisfaction theories. It is *God himself* who in Christ accomplishes the work of redemption and overcomes sin, death, and the devil. God himself entered the world of sin and death: "the same hand of God that formed us in the beginning, and forms us in our mother's womb, in these later days sought us when we were lost, gaining his lost sheep and laying it on his shoulders and bringing it back with joy to the flock of life."[16]

In a rather lengthy but moving passage Irenaeus explains how the Incarnate Son has sanctified each stage of life:

> He came to save all through his own person; all, that is, who through him are reborn to God; infants, children, boys, young men and old. Therefore he passed through every stage of life. He was made an infant for infants, sanctifying infancy; a child among children, sanctifying childhood, and setting an example of filial affection, of righteousness, and obedience; a young man among young men, becoming an example to them, and sanctifying them to the Lord. So also he was a grown man among the older men, that he might be a perfect teacher for all, not merely in respect to revelation of the truth, but also in respect to this stage of life, sanctifying the older men, and becoming an example to them also. And thus he came even to death, that he might be 'the firstborn from the dead,' having the pre-eminence among all, the Author of Life, who goes before all and shows the way.[17]

The divine victory accomplished in Christ is set at the very center of Irenaeus' thought and forms the central element of his doctrine of Recapitulation, the restoring and perfecting of creation, which is his most comprehensive theological idea. Aulén can say of the doctrine:

> The Recapitulation does not end with the triumph of Christ over the enemies which had held man in bondage; it continues in the work of the Spirit in the Church. . . . But

---

15. *Against Heresies.*
16. *Ibid.*, V, 15.a
17. *Ibid.*, II, xxii. 4.

the completeness of the Recapitulation is not realised in this life: Irenaeus' outlook is strongly eschatological, and the gift of the Spirit is for him the earnest of future glory.[18]

For Irenaeus, therefore, while the death of Christ holds a central place in the divine victory, it is not death in isolation; as Aulén points out, "It is death in connection, on the one hand, with the life-work of Christ as a whole, and on the other with the Resurrection and Ascension; the death irradiated with the light of Easter and Pentecost."[19] The Resurrection was the first manifestation of Christ's decisive victory, which was won on the Cross; it was also the starting point for the new era of the Spirit, for exalted at the Father's right hand Christ pours out the Spirit who reproduces within us the victory of Christ over sin and brings us into "unity and communion with God and man."

It is against this background of Atonement doctrine that we understand Irenaeus' teaching of perfection. Christians are living in the new stage of salvation. "The essential fact in this new stage," Flew notes, "is the outpouring of the Spirit. Only those, he says, are 'perfect' in the sense of complete, who have received the Spirit of God. The thought of Irenaeus is always dominated by his strong conviction of a present communion of the soul with God. He knows well that this is what is meant by 'receiving the Spirit.'"[20]

Irenaeus' idea of Recapitulation, drawn from Eph. 1:10 and Col. 1:19, "is inherently a doctrine of perfection and . . . is at the heart of the theology of Irenaeus. That is the goal of our being—to be in Christ, and having received the Spirit, living in communion with God."[21] In the theologian's own words:

> God promised through the prophets to "pour out this Spirit upon his servants and handmaidens in the last days, that they may prophesy." And the Spirit descended from God on the Son of God, made son of man, and with him became accustomed to dwell among the human race and to "rest on" men and to dwell in God's creatures, working the Father's will in them and renewing them from their old state into the newness of Christ.[22]

---

18. Aulén, *Christus Victor*, p. 22.

19. *Ibid.*, p. 31.

20. R. Newton Flew, *The Idea of Perfection* (London: Oxford University Press, 1934), p. 125.

21. *Ibid.*, p. 127.

22. *Against Heresies*, III, xvii. 1.

Therefore Irenaeus is able to say, "God is mighty to make that perfect which the willing spirit desires," and, "the Apostle calls them perfect who present body, soul, and spirit without blame before God; who not only have the Holy Spirit abiding in them, but also preserve faultless their souls and bodies, keeping their fidelity to God and fulfilling their duties to their neighbours."[23] He sums up his doctrine by saying simply that "the Son of God appeared on earth and was conversant with men: that we may be after the image and likeness of God."[24]

---

23. Quoted by Pope, *Christian Theology*, 3:62.
24. *Demonstration*, c. 97 (149-50).

CHAPTER 4

The Christian Platonists

In Irenaeus we hear the voice of the apostle Paul. His writings show the influence of Greek thought, to be sure, but they breathe with the true apostolic spirit. Beyond all question, Irenaeus was a biblical thinker, and his doctrine of Christian Perfection is an outgrowth of his profound grasp of God's atoning work in Christ Jesus.

In the writings of the men we shall now consider—Clement of Alexandria and his successor, Origen—we discern an entirely different tone and emphasis. In them, especially in Origen, we hear the voice of Plato as much as the voice of Paul. While both men were steeped in the knowledge of Holy Scripture, believed in Christ and loved Him supremely, their writings breathe the spirit of Greek philosophy. The perfection they teach, while informed by the mind of Jesus and of Paul, is a Christian transformation of the ideal of perfect virtue and goodness found in the dialogues of Plato. For them, the perfect man is the "Christian Gnostic," the man whose knowledge of God has enabled him to subdue his human passions and live a life of Christian virtue. For this reason Clement and Origen have been called "the Christian Platonists."

These men were addressing the message of Christ to the educated people of Alexandria, the second city of the Roman Empire. Founded by Alexander the Great in 332 B.C., it was primarily a commercial city and, as such, attracted large numbers of Greeks and Jews. Its intellectual life was no less remarkable. Its libraries were the most famous in the empire. On its streets East and West met. There Greek philosophy had already been wed to Judaism in the thought of Philo, a contemporary of Jesus, and there the Old Testament had been translated into Greek. We do not know when Christianity was introduced into Alexandria, but it must have been early, since it was strongly rooted there by the second century.

It is this deep blending of Greek philosophy and biblical faith, so characteristic of Alexandrian thought for more than two centuries, which finds expression in the perfectionist teaching of Clement and Origen.

A. Clement of Alexandria

Titus Flavius Clemens was born about 150, most probably in Athens. His intimate knowledge of Greek literature and customs is rivalled only by his equally intimate knowledge of the Bible. Mondésert says, "The Bible . . . became for him almost a language and a mentality; and what is strange, one can say the same about Greek philosophy and above all, Platonism."[1]

Clement wrote three treatises on Christian perfection, *Paedagogus, Protrepticus,* and *Stromateis. Paedagogus* means "Instructor" and has been titled "Christ the Educator" in *The Fathers of the Church.*[2] *Protrepticus* is commonly called "An Exhortation to the Greeks." *Stromateis* is not meant to be a finished treatise; as the term suggests, it is a collection of random thoughts. In *Paedagogus* Clement speaks of the perfection of religious experience which every believer enjoys in Christ. In *Protrepticus* he makes a glowing appeal to the Greeks to recognize all the truth and beauty praised by their poets and philoso-

---

1. C. Mondésert, *Clément d'Alexandrie* (Paris: 1944), p. 265.
2. Ed. Roy Joseph Deferrari (New York: 1954).

phers in the New Song which is Christ. Finally, in *Stromateis* he sets out to develop the higher perfection which the "Christian Gnostic" finds in Christ.

1. *The Perfect Life*

For Clement, to believe in Christ is to experience an initial perfection. "When we are reborn, we straightway receive the perfection for which we strive. For we were enlightened, that is, we came to the knowledge of God. Certainly, he who possesses knowledge of the Perfect Being is not imperfect."[3] This is the perfection of all genuine Christian experience, the knowledge of God, which is life eternal (cf. 1 John 1:5).

The new birth is also an ethical experience. "By the divine Spirit we get rid of the sins which dim our eyes like a mist, and leave the eye of the spirit free and unhindered and enlightened. By this eye alone we behold God, when the Holy Spirit pours into us from Heaven."[4] Clement is insistent that all who are born of God must "to the best of their ability be as sinless as they can. . . . There is nothing more important for us than first to be rid of sin and weakness, and then to uproot any habitual sinful inclination."[5]

Clement is clear in his understanding that Christ must first heal us from the disease of sin before He can teach us the way of higher perfection.

> If a person is sick, he cannot master any of the things taught him until he is first completely cured. We give instructions to some one who is sick for an entirely different reason than we do for some one who is learning; the latter, we instruct that he may acquire knowledge, the first, that he may regain health. Just as our body needs a physician when it is sick, so, too, when we are weak, our soul needs the Educator to cure its ills. Only then does it need the Teacher to guide and develop its capacity to know, once it is made pure and capable of retaining the revelation of the Word.[6]

This is the hallowing of the common life. Flew can say, "There are few of the Christian writers of that age, or indeed of any age, who see with such clearness as Clement that the gift of

---

3. Simon P. Wood, *Christ the Educator* (Fathers of the Church, Inc.: 1954), p. 25.

4. *Paedagogus*, I. vi (28).

5. *Christ the Educator*, p. 5.

6. *Ibid.*

communion with God brings with it not only a reinforcement of heavenly virtues, but also a transformation of the common task. Clement is depicting as an ideal a life that can be lived in Alexandria, amid a busy, commercial, pleasure-loving, and excitable population."[7]

Clement knows there is a Christian way of life, a gracious and Christlike behavior, which comes as a natural fruit of the new relationship with God. This new way of life is described in detail in the *Paedagogus*. But rarely has the transformation of grace been so beautifully described as in the famous passage of *Protrepticus:*

> It is his nature, as man, to be in close fellowship with God. As then we do not force the horse to plough, nor the bull to hunt, but lead each animal to its natural work; for the same reason we call upon man, who was made for the contemplation of heaven, and is in truth a heavenly plant, to come to the knowledge of God. . . . Have you found God? You have life.[8]

2. *The Christian Gnostic*

For Clement, salvation is the entire work of God which begins with the divine persuasion of prevenient grace, becomes actual in the rebirth of the Spirit, which in turn opens the way for the higher knowledge of perfect love which he terms *gnosis* (hereafter called Gnosis or knowledge).

It is essential that we distinguish Clement's Gnosis from that of pagan Gnosticism. The pagan Gnosis is an esoteric knowledge possible only for a select few who are *by nature* "the spiritual" *(pneumatikoi).* For the pagan Gnostic "the perfect" are a predestined few; for Clement true Gnosis is a possibility for all Christians.

The truth is, the *Logos*—the divine Word who was incarnate in Jesus—has been training all men everywhere in the way of true knowledge and life. "Our instructor is the holy God, Jesus, the Word who is the guide of all humanity."

> God is the source of all good; either directly, as in the Old and New Testaments, or indirectly, as in the case of philosophy. But it may be that philosophy was given to the Greeks directly; for it was "a schoolmaster," to bring Hellenism to

---

7. Flew, *Idea of Perfection,* p. 139.
8. *Protrepticus,* X.

Christ, as the Law was for the Hebrews. Thus philosophy was a preparation, paving the way for the man who is brought to perfection by Christ.[9]

The training of humanity by the Word has been, therefore, a progressive education. So it is also in the Church. "The all-loving Word, anxious to perfect us in a way that leads progressively to salvation, makes effective use of an order well adapted to our development; at first, He persuades, then He educates, and after all this He teaches."[10]

"Faith," or simple trust in Christ, is sufficient for salvation; but the man who to his faith adds "knowledge" has a higher possession. He is the true Christian Gnostic.

"To him who has shall be given"; to faith, knowledge; to knowledge, love; and to love, the inheritance. . . . This knowledge leads to the end, the endless final end, *a life of conformity to God*. . . . Thus being set free, those who have been perfected are given their reward. They have done with their purification, they have done with the rest of their service, though it be a holy service, with the holy; now they have become pure in heart, and because of their close intimacy with the Lord there awaits them a restoration to eternal contemplation.[11]

Flew comments on Clement's two levels of perfection as follows: "The perfection to which believers are called by the *Stromateis* is *theoría*, a full unification of the powers of the soul. There is knowledge in it but there is also love, complete harmony of purpose and desire. The first kind of perfection[12] leads naturally to the second because the second is already given and implicit in the first."[13]

The Gnosis of which Clement speaks is not mere intellectual knowledge. "It is a kind of perfection of man as man, harmonious and consistent with itself and with the divine Word, being completed both as to the disposition and the manner of life and speech, by the science of divine things. For it is by insight that faith is made perfect."[14] Clement is now thinking of God, not in

---

9. *Stromateis*, I, v (28, 1).

10. *Ibid.*, iii.

11. *Ibid.*, VII, x (italics added).

12. The perfection of the *Paedagogus*—knowing God through faith in Chirst.

13. Flew, *Idea of Perfection*, pp. 141-42.

14. *Stromateis*, V. i.

43

Platonic but in Christian terms. *Christian Perfection in its highest reaches is communion with God and "conformity to God." It is purity of heart, intimacy with God who is Love.*

> God is himself love, and because of his love he pursued us. . . . It was in his love that the Father pursued us, and the great proof of this is the Son whom he begot from himself and the love that was the fruit produced from his love. . . . And when he gave himself as a ransom, he left us a new testament: "I give you my love" (John 13:34). What is the nature and extent of this love? For each of us he laid down his life, the life which was worth the whole universe, and he requires in return that we should do the same for each other.[15]

It follows that the Gnosis which the Christian seeks involves not only the knowledge and love of God but *ethical perfection.* The final statement of Gnosis in the seventh book of the *Stromateis* is conclusive that Clement is at one with Paul in regarding love as the goal of the Christian life. He lays stress on the disinterestedness of perfect love. It is serving God from sheer devotion to His goodness and doing good, not to be seen of men, but to reflect the image and likeness of the Lord. He who shows mercy ought not to know that he shows mercy! Says Flew, "Such mercy will be a habit (éxis), a disposition (diáthesis), and this lovely freedom from self-consciousness is the soul's ideal."[16]

This perfection is not an achievement of man; it is the work of the Teaching Word, a gift from God to the Christian who has learned to pray without ceasing. Perfection is the work of Christ, the Word who dwells in the heart.

> If prayer is thus an occasion for communion with God, no occasion for our approach to God must be neglected. Certainly the holiness of the gnostic, being bound up with the Divine Providence through a voluntary acknowledgement on his part, shows the beneficence of God in perfection. For the holiness of the gnostic is, as it were, a return back on itself of Providence, and a responsive feeling of loyalty on the part of the friend of God.[17]

A return back on itself of Providence! This phrase expresses clearly the ultimate truth that *all things are of God* in the life of the believer who is being perfected. The "perfect" Christian acknowledges that a beneficent Providence is shaping his

---

15. *Quis Dives Salvetur*, 37.

16. Flew, *Idea of Perfection*, p. 145 (quoting *Stromateis*, iv. 22. 135-38).

17. *Stromateis*, VI. xlii.

destiny and transforming him into the likeness of Christ (cf. Rom. 8:28-29).

To grasp something of Clement's vision of perfection is to understand why Alexander Knox could write of John Wesley: "To realize in himself the perfect Christian of Clemens Alexandrinus was the object of his heart."

B. Origen

Clement's most celebrated pupil and his successor as head of the catechetical school in Alexandria was the renowned Origen (c. 185-255). Like Clement he had been a student of both Christian Scripture and Greek philosophy from childhood. According to Jerome he wrote 6,000 books! Even if we discount this number drastically, he was one of the most voluminous writers of the ancient world. He was a biblical critic and commentator and wrote the first systematic work on Christian theology.

In agreement with Clement, Origen drew a sharp distinction between "faith" and "knowledge," but he interpreted both differently. For Origen, faith is the acceptance of the essential Christian doctrines, and knowledge, the demonstration of them. *Faith saves, but knowledge perfects.* He based his doctrine of Gnosis on what Paul wrote in the 12th chapter of First Corinthians:

> Moreover it should be known that the holy apostles in preaching the faith of Christ spoke most clearly on certain matters which they believed to be necessary for all believers, even for those who seemed slow in investigating divine science; but left the reason for their statements to be inquired into by those who have received the excellent gifts of the Spirit, particularly the gifts of language, wisdom, and knowledge.[18]

To accept Christian beliefs is to be saved; to go on to a knowledge of the further truth deduced from these beliefs and from Scripture is to have Gnosis and achieve perfection.

To ascend the summit of Christian perfection one must turn his back on the outward visible world as well as upon the emotions of mankind. When one enters the secret chamber of wisdom and knowledge he closes the door upon all things per-

---

18. *De principiis*, pref. 3.

ceived by the senses. The "perfect" Christian is one who, like Moses, has ascended above all created things.[19]

For those who would press on to perfection, Origen's first advice was, "Know thyself." This means to recognize that the body itself with its desires and emotions must be overcome. The Christian is engaged in a ceaseless struggle with the hindering body as he pursues the perfect knowledge of God and the perfect spiritual Gnosis. He must therefore employ the weapons of asceticism if he is to win the victory over his lower self. "Paul's saying, *I buffet my body,* is interpreted in this sense," Flew comments. "The words of Jesus (except ye . . . become as little children) means the mortifying of the lusts of mankind, because the child has not tasted sexual pleasure."[20]

Commenting on Matthew's account of the Transfiguration, Origen interprets the phrase "after six days" (Matt. 17:1) to mean passing beyond created things, for the world was created in six days. If anyone would be deemed worthy to behold the Transfiguration he must pass beyond the six days and no longer behold the things of the world. Then he will observe a new Sabbath and rejoice on the high mountain of God.[21]

The ladder to perfection is climbed gradually. The Christian knows no sudden break with sin. Conversion is only a return of the will to the will of God. Salvation from sin begins with baptism, where one ceases to be a sinner. The baptized Christian is no longer a servant of sin; he sins, but he is not a sinner.[22] With the help of God he gradually conquers his sins and makes definite progress toward the conquest of moral evil.[23]

Answering those who deny the possibility of moral perfection, Origen says:

> Human nature by the exercise of will has acquired the ability to walk on a tight-rope suspended high in the theatre . . . and it has achieved this ability by practice and application: Are we to suppose that it is impossible for human nature to live virtuously, if it so wills, even if it has formerly sunk very low? A man who says this is surely bringing an indictment against the character of the Creator of the rational

---

19. *Contra Celsus,* i. 19.
20. Flew, *Idea of Perfection,* p. 153.
21. *Comm. Matt.* xii. 36.
22. *Comm. Rom.* v. 5.
23. *Ibid.,* 8.

46

being rather than against the creature. For he is suggesting that he has made human nature competent to achieve things that are difficult but of no use, but incompetent to attain his own true blessedness.[24]

Even though the achievement of this perfection is not possible without the accompanying assistance of God's grace, the scheme is essentially humanistic. Man takes the initiative, and God assists. Origen explains: "Man's will is not sufficient to attain the end [of salvation], nor is the running of the metaphorical athletes competent to attain 'the prize of the upward summons of God in Christ Jesus.' This is only accomplished by God's assistance. . . . Our perfection does not come about by our remaining inactive, yet it is not accomplished by our own activity; God plays the greater part in effecting it."[25]

Origen clearly intends to ascribe perfection to the grace of God: "In respect of our salvation, 'The will and the activity come from God.'"[26] But in explaining *how* this is true, he betrays a failure to grasp the New Testament doctrine of grace —that in our salvation the initiative is entirely of God. Origen's is a doctrine of "free will" rather than "free grace." Even though fallen man is hampered by sin, "human nature by the exercise of will" is "competent to attain true blessedness." All that is needed is the *assistance* of God. The initiative is not God's but man's. It is an anthropocentric rather than a theocentric understanding of salvation.

In the teaching of Origen, therefore, the doctrine of Christian Perfection takes "a fatal step,"[27] substituting for biblical premises the presuppositions of Greek philosophy.

1. For Origen, faith is not personal trust but mental assent to truth. Inevitably salvation becomes a matter of human effort. The Gnosis which the perfect Christian receives is intellectual rather than spiritual.

2. The negative evaluation of the human body is Platonic and not biblical; perfection thus comes through victory over the body. Inevitably, sin comes to be understood in terms of sex desire. Because of the fall of Adam, our body is "the body of

---

24. *Contra Celsus*, iii. 69.
25. *De principiis*, III. i. 18.
26. *Ibid.*, 19.
27. Flew, *Idea of Perfection*, p. 151.

sin." It is in the sex act itself that sin is propagated, through the seed of the male. Christ therefore had no "body of sin" because He "was not conceived by means of the seed of a man."[28] "Thus every man is polluted in father and mother and only Jesus my Lord came to birth without stain."[29] In Augustine this doctrine reached full flower, as we shall see, with Original Sin being virtually identified with lust or concupiscence, which while not limited to sexual desire is most vividly understood as such.

3. Perfection becomes the soul's mystic ascent of the "Sacred Ladder." It is not the gift of God's *agape* for man, received by faith through grace; it is the expression of *eros*, the fulfillment of man's love for God, and hence the achievement of man who is only assisted by divine grace. Although Origen refers to the Holy Spirit as our Sanctifier, in the passage in *De principiis* where he makes this point he does not relate sanctification of the Spirit to the redemptive work of Christ. McGiffert can say, "The truth is that Origen's mind was in confusion of the whole subject of salvation as it was concerning the work of the Holy Spirit."[30] In his confusion he sacrifices the New Testament teaching that our salvation is from first to last entirely and solely by the grace of God.

4. Finally Origen opened the door to monasticism with its idea of perfection through asceticism and the consequent notion of a double standard of Christian life. Taking Jesus' words in Matthew 19:12 as a counsel of perfection, Origen had himself emasculated in order to become a "eunuch for the kingdom of heaven's sake"! The time was ripe for those who wished to be "perfect" to escape the world and "mortify" their bodies. Since the rank and file who must remain in the workaday world could not heed the counsel of perfection, they were left to struggle along in a life of imperfection and sin. "Probably the most unfortunate aspect of this double idea," Walker thinks, "was that it tended to discourage the efforts of the ordinary Christian."[31]

---

28. *Comm. Rom.* v. 9.

29. *Hom. in Leviticum*, xii. 4.

30. McGiffert, *History of Christian Thought*, 1:221.

31. Williston Walker, *A History of the Christian Church* (New York: Chas. Scribner's Sons, 1944), p. 104.

CHAPTER 5

Monastic Perfection

In apostolic times the Church was undoubtedly conceived as composed exclusively of experiential Christians. There were those in it who needed discipline, as a reading of the New Testament Epistles reveals, but the ideal was of the Church as "not having spot or wrinkle or any such thing."

The growth of Christianity in the empire, however, diluted this concept of a holy church. By the beginning of the third century there were many whose parents, possibly remote ancestors, had been experiential Christians but who, though they attended public worship, were Christians in little more than name.

In the third and fourth centuries the church grew rapidly and became increasingly worldly. As common Christian practice grew less strenuous, asceticism grew in the thought of the serious. The *Didache,* a church manual drawn up in the first half of the second century, urged: "If thou art able to bear the whole yoke of the Lord, thou shalt be perfect; but if thou art not able, do that which thou art able."

The tendency toward a separation between the higher and lower Christian life was greatly furthered by a distinction clearly drawn by Tertullian and Origen, between the "advice" and "requirements" of the gospel. While the requirements are binding on all Christians, the advice is for those who would truly be holy.

Christ said to the rich young ruler, "If thou wouldest be perfect, go, sell that thou hast, and give to the poor, and thou shalt have treasure in heaven" (Matt. 19:21). He also declared that some are "eunuchs for the kingdom of heaven's sake" (Matt. 19:12), and that "in the resurrection they neither marry nor are given in marriage" (Matt. 22:30). Paul had written "to the unmarried and to widows, it is good for them to remain even as I" (1 Cor. 7:8). These scriptures were taken quite literally by those who yearned for true holiness; but obviously voluntary poverty and voluntary celibacy were deemed advice the average Christian could not fulfill. As we shall see, these texts became the foundation stones for monasticism and Christian asceticism.

The conversion of Constantine and the recognition of Christianity as the official religion of the empire led to a vast influx of pagan church members and, in turn, to an enhanced valuation of the ascetic life by serious-minded Christians. The cessation of martyrdom left the ascetic life as the highest Christian achievement. The world was filled with sights and practices that offended the Christian conscience, from which it seemed right to flee. And the mentality of antiquity favored the practice of contemplation above the active life. But above all, the formalism of public worship which developed by the close of the third century, led to a desire for a freer and more individual approach to God.

Such appear to have been the powerful forces which gave birth to the monastic movement. At the heart of monasticism was the yearning to recover the lost purity and power of the Christian faith, to give close and serious attention to Christ's call to perfection. R. Newton Flew claims that "Monasticism is the boldest organized attempt to attain to Christian perfection in all the long history of the Church."[1]

A. Beginnings of Monasticism

Anthony, the father of monasticism, was a native of the vil-

---

1. Flew, *Idea of Perfection,* p. 158.

lage of Koma in central Egypt. Athanasius tells that Anthony was on his way to church and was distressed by the thought of his own unworthiness, as compared to the apostles, who had left all to follow Christ. It happened that the Gospel of the day was the word of Jesus to the young ruler: "If thou wouldest be perfect . . . !" Anthony's hour had come. He sold all he had and purchased his freedom "from the chains of the world." This was about the year 270.

At first Anthony took up an ascetic life in his native village, but 15 years later he went into solitude and became a monk. "He confirmed his purpose not to return to the abode of his fathers, nor to the remembrance of his kinfolk; but to keep all his desire and energy for perfecting his discipline."[2]

The soil of monasticism was undoubtedly prepared by many movements of the mind—the thought of bodily life as evil, the ideal of the contemplative life as superior to active practice, the neo-Platonic yearning for the beatific vision—but the seed itself is easily recognizable. And it was "sown by those busily at work in the garden of the church."

Anthony's aim was to attain perfection. He set himself to win the virtues he had seen in others, and by a ceaseless life of prayer to find true communion with God. To read the other early documents of monasticism is to find the same quest for perfection. The monastics of the church—Pachomius, Basil, Benedict, and much later Francis of Assisi—heard the same call to perfection.

B. The Monastic Ideals

For the Christian monk there were only two realities, God and his own soul, his soul and God. Monasticism was the religion of the solitary soul with God.

One of Anthony's pivotal texts was, "The kingdom of heaven is within you." Other writers expanded the idea. The goal of the spiritual life is the kingdom of God, which means purity of heart. To become perfect one must renounce the world, combat the flesh and wage war against sin to the death; but the summit of perfection is prayer, prayer without ceasing.

While the life of contemplation and communion remained

---

2. *Vit. Ant.*, i. 3.

an ideal of monasticism, many saw the solitary life as making possible a fruitful life of service to one's fellowmen. Basil, in fact, takes issue with the idea of the solitary life as an end in itself:

> The fashion of the love of Christ does not allow us to look each at his own good. For "love," we read, "seeketh not its own." Now the solitary life has one aim, the service of the needs of the individual. But this is plainly in conflict with the law of love, which the apostle fulfilled when he sought not his own advantage, but that of the many, that they might be saved.[3]

As against Basil, Cassian advocated the superiority of the solitary life. Through Thomas Aquinas the conception of the solitary life as ultimately superior became current in the Roman Catholic church. But Chrysostom and Jerome, in the Eastern church, followed the lead of Basil.

Another mark of the monastic ideal is the cross. The monk took up his cross to follow Jesus. Basil's attitude toward renunciation is typical. After quoting Matt. 17:24, Luke 14:33 and 26, he writes:

> Accordingly perfect renunciation consists in a man's attaining complete impassivity as regards actual living, and having "the sentence of death," so as to put no confidence in himself. Whereas its beginnings consist of alienation from external things, such as possessions, vainglory, the common customs of life, or attachment to useless things . . . So he who is seized by the vehement desire of following Christ can no longer care for anything to do with this life.

But Basil offers a corrective and makes it clear that the final goal of renunication is knowing and gaining Christ. He quotes, as one who understands, the word of Paul: "For whom I suffered the loss of all things and do count them but dung, that I may win Christ." "Greatest of all," Basil comments, "renunciation is the beginning of our being made like unto Christ." The goal is "love towards God, which both stirs us up to work the Lord's commandments and is in its turn preserved by them in permanence and security."[4]

The finest proof of the desire to enter into communion with Christ crucified is the passion which breathes through the closing sections of the *Moralia:*

---

3. Flew, *Idea of Perfection*, p. 164.
4. *Reg. fus. tract.*, 8. 350D; 5. 342C.

What is the mark of a Christian? To be cleansed from all pollution of the flesh and spirit, in the blood of Christ. . . .

What is the mark of those who eat the bread and drink the cup of the Lord? To keep in perpetual memory Him who died for us and rose again.

What is the mark of those that keep such a memory? To live unto themselves no longer, but unto Him who died for them and rose again.

What is the mark of a Christian? That his righteousness should abound in everything, more than that of the Scribes and Pharisees, according to the measure of the teaching of the Lord in the Gospel.

What is the mark of a Christian? To love one another, even as Christ also loved us.

What is the mark of a Christian? To see the Lord always before him.

What is the mark of a Christian? To watch each night and day in the perfection of pleasing God to be ready, knowing that the Lord cometh at an hour he thinketh not.[5]

There can be no doubt that Basil believed that the heart could in this life be purified from sin and that the commandments of love could be kept.[6] Of Basil, W. K. Lowther Clarke has written: "He believes intensely in sanctification. In and by the Spirit, the Christian living under the favourable conditions of a monastery, can avoid sin."

In the rules of Basil and Benedict, the ideal of perfection is socialized. It is unfair to judge monasticism by its extremely individualistic expressions or to think of it only in the degenerate forms castigated by the Protestant reformers.

We must not forget that it was the Benedictines who became the missionaries of Europe. In the more mature forms of monasticism the ideal mission of the monks was that of the Old Testament remnant: to aid the church in its task of purifying itself and evangelizing the world. Paul Tillich has rightly pointed out: "Monasticism represents the uncompromising negation of the world, but this negation was not a quietistic one. It was a negation coupled with activity directed toward transforming the world—in labor, science, and other forms of culture, church architecture and building, poetry and music. It was a very interesting phenomenon and has little to do with the deteriorated monasticism against which the Reformers and humanists were

---

5. *Moralia,* 1xx. 22; 318B, C.
6. *Reg. brev. tract.,* 280, 296.

fighting. On the one hand, it was a radical movement of resignation from the world; but on the other hand, it did not fall merely into a mystical form of asceticism; it applied itself to the transformation of reality."[7]

C. Macarius the Egyptian

The "Homilies of Macarius the Egyptian" may be taken as representative of the monastic ideal of perfection. Although little known today, they have had their influence upon the history of perfection. William Law read them with admiration, and John Wesley published extracts from them in the first volume of his *Christian Library,* a series designed to nourish the early Methodists in the finest writings of the saints.[8]

In his original condition, Macarius taught, man was clothed with the glory of God as with a garment. That glory has been forfeited by sin, but is now restored to the saints by the gift of the Divine Spirit. "The inward man may be made partaker of that glory in this present life and have that holiness of the Spirit" which will envelop our very bodies in the Resurrection when Christ comes to catch us away.[9]

The perfection of the saints is "the irradiation and presence of the Holy Spirit, which is unspeakable, and the mystical fellowship in the fulness of grace."[10] The hope of the soul is "an entire redemption from sin and the darkness of the affections: that being purified by the Spirit, sanctified in soul and body, it may be made a vessel clean and prepared for the susception of the heavenly ointment, and the residence of Christ, the true and heavenly King. And then is the soul filled with the heavenly life and becomes the pure habitation of the Holy Spirit."[11]

Macarius' doctrine of perfection was grounded in the Incar-

---

7. Paul Tillich, *A History of Christian Thought,* ed. by Carl Braaten (New York and Evanston: Harper and Row, Publishers, 1968), p. 145.

8. Unless otherwise indicated, all references to the Homilies are from John Wesley's *A Christian Library,* "Consisting of Extracts from and Abridgements of the Choicest Pieces of Practical Divinity which have been published in the English Tongue. In Thirty Volumes. By John Wesley. Vol. I. London: T. Cordeus, 1819."

9. *Homilies,* IV. 9.

10. *Ibid.,* 2.

11. *Ibid.,* 3.

nation. Because God has come to us in Christ we may receive the sanctifying Spirit and be perfected.

The soul is surnamed the temple and habitation of God, for the Scripture says, *I will dwell in them and walk in them.* So it pleased God; because He came down from the holy heavens and embraced thy reasonable nature, the flesh, which is of the earth, and mingled it with His divine Spirit, in order that thou, the earthy, mightest receive the heavenly soul. And when thy soul has communion with the Spirit and the heavenly soul enters thy soul, then thou art a perfect man in God, and an heir, and a son.[12]

"These are heights which the soul does not reach all at once; but through many labours and conflicts, with variety of trials and temptations, it receives spiritual growth and improvement, till at last it comes to an entire exemption from its old affections."[13] The person who desires to become "the mansion-house of Christ and to be filled with the Holy Spirit, so that he may bring forth the fruits of the Spirit and perform the commandments of Christ in purity, ought to begin first with believing in the Lord, to give himself entirely up to the directions of his commandments, and to bid an universal farewell to the world."[14]

The man who thus comes to Christ is born of God, becomes a new man. Macarius then quotes 2 Cor. 5:17: "If any man be in Christ, he is a new creature."

For our Lord Jesus Christ came for this very reason, that he might change, and renew, and *create afresh* this soul that had been perverted by vile affections, tempering it with his own Divine Spirit. He came to work a new mind, and a new soul, and new eyes, new ears, and a new spiritual tongue; yea, to make them that believe in him *new men,* that he might *pour* into them the *new wine,* which is his Spirit.[15]

But while this first change is miraculous and transforming, "there is yet a remnant of corruption" in the believer.[16] However, "the unsteady and unskilful, imagine presently they have no more sin. Whereas they that have discretion cannot deny

---

12. Cited by Flew, *Idea of Perfection,* p. 182. Wesley's abridgement omits this quotation.

13. *Homilies,* VI. 4.

14. *Ibid.,* XI. 1.

15. *Ibid.,* XIX. 1.

16. *Ibid.,* VIII. 2.

that even we who have the grace of God may be molested again with evil thoughts. For we have often instances of some among the brethren, that have experienced such a degree of joy and grace, as to affirm, that for five or six years running, they had no sin in them; and yet after all, when they thought themselves freed entirely from it, the corruption lurked within, was stirred up anew, and they were well nigh burnt up."[17] John Wesley cites this quotation in his sermon on "The Scripture Way of Salvation," in support of his doctrine of sin in believers.[18]

The Christian who would be filled with the Spirit must not only "have discretion" to recognize his remaining sin; "he ought ever to continue instant in prayer, in the faith and expectation of the Lord, waiting at all times for his help, with the full bent of his mind fixed upon it."[19] And he must "force himself" to a single-hearted obedience to the commandments of the Lord, "setting the Lord ever before his eyes, desirous of pleasing him only, in meekness of heart." But eventually "the things which he does now by violence, and with a reluctant heart, he will in time do freely. . . . For the Lord . . . shows mercy to him and redeems him from his enemies and from the sin that dwelleth in him, *filling him with the Spirit.* And thus for the future, without compulsion or difficulty, does he perform the commands of the Lord in truth. Or rather, the Lord himself doth his own commandments in him; and then he brings forth the fruits of the Spirit in purity."[20]

When the Spirit has come in His fullness He teaches the Christian "the true prayer, the true love, the true meekness— which before he forced himself to, and sought after, and which took up his whole thoughts."[21]

> Thus the commandments of God being fulfilled by us through his Spirit, and that Spirit perfecting us in itself, and being itself completed in us, when once cleansed from all the pollution and stain of sin, it will then present our souls to Christ as beautiful brides, pure and blameless; we, on the one hand, reposing ourselves in God, in his kingdom—and God, on the other, taking up his rest in us to endless ages![22]

---

17. *Ibid.,* IX. 4.
18. *Works,* 6:45-46.
19. *Homilies,* XI. 2.

20. *Ibid.,* 3, 4; also XI. 8.
21. *Ibid.,* 10.
22. *Ibid.,* 11.

Christian perfection, therefore, is to be "purified in heart by the Holy Ghost."[23]

> Let us therefore have faith in him, and come to him in truth, that he may speedily perform his healing operation within us:—for he hath promised to "give to them that ask him, his Holy Spirit; and to open to them that knock; and to be found of them that seek him:" and he that promised *cannot lie*. To him be glory for ever! Amen.[24]

The *Homilies* breathe this spirit of expectancy and confidence in the sanctifying grace of God. Quotation upon quotation could be cited to prove that Macarius taught a doctrine of inward sanctification which anticipates at almost every point the Wesleyan teaching. For the Egyptian, God's grace in Christ is sufficient to restore man to the holiness he lost through Adam's transgression. Indeed, the very purpose of redemption is "to restore to thee the original formation of Adam in his purity."

> Q. Is the natural concupiscence rooted out by the coming of the Holy Spirit?
>
> A. Sin is rooted out, and man receives the original formation of Adam in his purity. Through the power of the Spirit he comes up to the first Adam; yea, is made greater than him (sic).
>
> Q. Is Satan let loose to a certain degree, or makes he war as he pleases? . . .
>
> A. Satan at no time sleeps. As long as any one lives in this world, and wears flesh, he finds war. But . . . Christians are clothed with the Spirit and are at rest. And though war ariseth from without, they are inwardly fortified with the power of the Lord. . . . Though outwardly they are tempted, yet inwardly are they filled with the Divine nature, and so nothing injured.

However, Macarius admits that one who has not come to the perfect love of Christ "still inwardly retains the war. He is one hour refreshed in prayer, and another in a state of affliction. . . . He is yet but an infant." Echoing St. Paul in First Corinthians, Macarius continues, "Many of the brethren have had the gifts of healing, and revelation and prophecy; however, not having attained to perfect charity, the war came upon them, and they fell. Indeed, if any one comes to perfect love, he is forever after bound and captivated by grace. But if any one make

---

23. *Ibid.,* XII. 8.
24. *Ibid.*

but small advances toward this, he is still in bondage to fear, and to war, and to falling."[25]

It is interesting that Macarius speaks several times of the baptism with the Holy Spirit in reference to sanctification.

> Q. What is the meaning of those words, "Which eye hath not seen, nor ear heard, neither have they entered into the heart of man"?
>
> A. At that time the great men, and the righteous, and the kings, knew that the Redeemer was to come: but that his blood was to be poured out upon the cross, they neither knew nor had heard neither had it entered into their heart, that there was to be a baptism of fire and of the Holy Ghost, and that Christians were to receive the Comforter, and be clothed with power from on high, and be filled with the Godhead.[26]

In another Homily he says that "Among them [the Jews] baptism sanctified the flesh, but with us it is the baptism of the Holy Ghost and fire."[27] "We ought, therefore, to believe *with our whole heart* his unspeakable *promises, to love the Lord,* and to be industrious in all virtues, and to beg continually to receive *the promise of his Spirit* entirely and perfectly."[28]

In Macarius the mystical and the ethical are blended in a manner reminiscent of the New Testament. The perfect Christian is filled with the Holy Spirit and enjoys "the mystical fellowship in the fulness of grace," but the final proof that he is Spirit-filled is the love of which Paul speaks in 1 Corinthians 13.[29] And in language reminiscent of the apostle's in 2 Cor. 3:18, he writes of the Christian life as one long looking to Christ, who stamps His own image upon our hearts.

> As a portrait painter keeps an eye on the king's face and draws, and when the king's face is toward him he draws the portrait easily and well, . . . in like manner Christ, the good artist, for those who believe Him and gaze continually at Him, straightway portrays after His own image a heavenly man. . . . We must therefore gaze upon Him, believing and loving Him, throwing away all else and attending to Him, in

---

25. *Ibid.,* XIV. 1, 2, 4, 5; XV. 4. By "natural concupiscence" Macarius seems to mean the *totality* of illicit desires which plague the soul that has forfeited "the formation of Adam." Absent from the *Homilies* is any preoccupation with sex. Sin is viewed as selfishness in all its manifestations. In view of this section, and a number of similar quotations, it is difficult to see why Flew denies Macarius a doctrine of complete cleansing.

26. *Ibid.,* XV. 5. 28. *Ibid.,* XIX. 7 (italics his).
27. *Ibid.,* XXI. 3; cf XVIII. 6. 29. *Ibid.,* XV. 4.

order that He may paint His own heavenly image and send it into our souls, and thus wearing Christ, we may receive eternal life, and even here may have full assurance and be at rest.[30]

In Macarius, John Wesley discovered a spiritual compatriot. Small wonder we encounter in Wesley's diary the entry: "I read Macarius and sang!"[31]

D. Gregory of Nyssa

Albert Outler considers Gregory of Nyssa "the greatest of all Eastern Christian teachers of the quest for perfection." No survey of the doctrine should omit his contributions to the theme. He devoted two treatises to the subject, "On What It Means to Call Oneself a Christian" and "On Perfection." For Gregory, Christ is the Prototype of the Christian life, and the alternate title to his work on perfection is, "On What It Is Necessary for the Christian to Be." Virginia Callahan thinks the work might better have been entitled "Christ, the Model of Perfection," since the central portion of the work consists of a detailed analysis of some 30 references to Christ in the writings of Paul, "who, according to St. Gregory, knew more than any other person what Christ is and transformed his own soul by his imitation of Christ."[32]

---

30. Cited by Flew, *Idea of Perfection*, p. 182. Wesley's abridgement omits this quotation.

31. In Wesley's day it was accepted as fact that the Macarian *Homilies* were actually the work of Macarius the Egyptian (301-91). However, Roman Catholic scholar Werner Laeger has put forward the argument that the author was not the fourth-century Egyptian "desert father," but a fifth-century *Syrian* monk whose conception of the Christian life was drawn almost exclusively from Gregory of Nyssa. In the supposed writings of Macarius the Egyptian, according to this view, Wesley was actually in touch with Gregory of Nyssa, "the greatest of all Eastern Christian teachers of the quest for perfection" (Albert C. Outler, *John Wesley* [New York: Oxford University Press, 1964], p. 9, fn. 26). One discerns, however, a marked difference of spiritual tone between Macarius and Gregory. The *Homilies* are mystical, whereas the Gregorian treatises are more philosophical. While Gregory does not overlook the truth of participation in Christ, for him our Lord is more the *model* and *prototype* of perfection than the indwelling Christ who reproduces himself in the believer (Macarius's position). If indeed the *Homilies* are the work of an unknown fifth-century Syrian monk, the latter has transformed Gregory's thought in a remarkable way.

32. Virginia Callahan, *St. Gregory of Nyssa Ascetical Works*, "The Fathers of the Church" (Washington, D.C.: The Catholic University of America, 1967), p. 93. The following quotations from Gregory come from "On Perfection," translated by Callahan in this volume.

Among the Pauline texts Gregory quotes as having significance for the Christian seeking perfection are those which declare that Christ is "the power of God and the wisdom of God" (1 Cor. 1:24), "peace" (Eph. 2:14), "light inaccessible" in whom God dwells (1 Tim. 6:16), "sanctification and redemption" (1 Cor. 1:30), "the brightness of glory and the image of substance" (Heb. 1:3), "spiritual food" (1 Cor. 10:30) and "spiritual drink and spiritual rock" (1 Cor. 10:4), "head of the body of the Church" (cf. Col. 1:18), "the firstborn of every creature" (Col. 1:15), "firstborn among many brethren" (Rom. 8:29), "firstborn from the dead" (Col. 1:18), "mediator between God and man" (1 Tim. 2:5), "only begotten Son" (John 3:16), and "lord of glory" (cf. 1 Cor. 2:8).[33]

Gregory's thesis is, "It is necessary . . . for those calling themselves after Christ, first of all, to become what the name implies, and, then, to adapt themselves to the title."[34] Those marks which we cannot imitate we reverence and worship. "Thus, it is necessary for the Christian life to illustrate all the interpretative terms signifying Christ, some through imitation, others through worship, if 'the man of God is to be perfect,' as the apostle says."[35]

In developing the theme, Gregory warns against a Christian remaining "double-natured, a centaur made up of reason and passion," and he cites Paul's question, "What fellowship hath light with darkness?" as an argument that the person containing these opposites becomes an enemy to himself, being divided in two ways between virtue and evil" and thus "sets up an antagonistic battle line with himself."[36] Several times he refers to this "civil war" which can only be resolved "through the death of my enemy," i.e., remaining sin.[37]

Referring to Christ as "the power of God and the wisdom of God," he observes that a person who prays draws into himself and looks toward Christ ("who is power") and "'is strengthened with power in the inner man,' as the apostle says, and the person calling upon the wisdom which is the Lord . . . becomes wise."[38]

Christ becomes our "peace" not only when He reconciles

---

33. "On Perfection," pp. 96-7.
34. *Ibid.*, p. 98.
35. *Ibid.*, p. 99.

36. *Ibid.*, p. 100.
37. *Ibid.*, p. 102.
38. *Ibid.*

"those fighting against on the outside, but also the elements at variance within us, in order that no longer may the 'flesh lust against the spirit and the spirit against the flesh.'"[39] "The definition of peace is the harmony of dissonant parts. Once the civil war in our nature is expelled, then we become peace and reveal our having taken on the name of Christ as true and authentic."[40]

"Knowing Christ as the 'true light,' it is necessary that our lives also be illuminated by the rays of . . . 'the Sun of Righteousness,' streaming forth for our illumination." "If we recognize Christ as our 'sanctification,' let us prove by our lives that we ourselves stand . . . with the power of his sanctification."[41]

Such thoughts as these are typical of Gregory's teaching of perfection. For him, the holy life is one in which the flesh, "which is hostile to God and not subject to the law of God," has been mortified in the consecration of "a living sacrifice, holy, pleasing to God," and the mind has been transformed, "that you may discern what is the good and acceptable and perfect will of God."[42] The perfect life, therefore, is "living in the flesh, but not 'according to the flesh.'"[43]

Although Gregory's theme is that of the imitation of Christ, he sees clearly the deeper truth of *participation* in Christ. This becomes clear in his exposition of Christ as the Head of the body (where "the separate parts" live "by communion with the head") and in his development of Christ as the Firstborn of every creature (who "has formed our life"). In connection with the latter image Gregory reminds us that we who have been "reborn 'by water and the Spirit'" and thereby "become brothers of the Lord" must reflect our Elder Brother in our daily life. "But what have we learned from Scripture that the character of His life is? What we have said many times, that, 'He committed no sin, nor was deceit found in his mouth.' Therefore, if we are going to act as brothers of the One who gave us birth, the sinlessness of our life will be a pledge of our relationship to Him."[44]

Finally, coming to the figure of Christ as the spiritual Rock, Gregory comments:

> Drawing from Him as from a pure and uncorrupted

---

39. *Ibid.*, pp. 102-3.
40. *Ibid.*, p. 103.
41. *Ibid.*

42. *Ibid.*, pp. 104-5.
43. *Ibid.*, p. 110.
44. *Ibid.*, p. 115.

stream, a person will show in his thoughts such a resemblance to his Prototype as exists between the water in the running stream and the water taken away from there in a jar. For the purity in Christ and the purity seen in the person who has a share in Him are the same, the one being the stream and the other drawn from it.[45]

"This, therefore, is perfection in the Christian life, . . . the participation of one's soul and speech and activities in all the names by which Christ is signified, so that the perfect holiness, according to the eulogy of Paul, is taken upon oneself in 'the whole body and soul and spirit,' continuously safeguarding against being mixed with evil."[46]

The Christian life which is being perfected is one in which the Christian is exchanging "glory for glory, becoming greater through daily increase, ever perfecting himself, and never arriving too quickly at the limit of perfection. For this truly is perfection, never to stop growing toward what is better and never placing any limit on perfection."[47]

---

45. *Ibid.*, p. 121.
46. *Ibid.*
47. *Ibid.*, p. 122.

CHAPTER **6**

Augustine

Some have questioned whether Augustine should be numbered among the advocates of Christian perfection. The fact is, he can be quoted by both friends and opponents of this truth.

Wiley lists Augustine among the witnesses to the doctrine. As evidence he cites the latter's statement that "no one should dare to say that God cannot destroy the original sin in the members, and make Himself so present to the soul, that the old nature being entirely abolished, a life should be lived below as life will be lived in the eternal contemplation of Him above."[1] And on the third centenary of Francois de Sales, Pope Pius XI, in an encyclical on holiness, stated: "St. Augustine puts the matter clearly when he says: 'God does not command the impossible, but in giving the commandment, He admonishes us to

---

1. Wiley, *Christian Theology*, 2:449-50.

accomplish what we can according to our strength, and to ask aid to accomplish whatever exceeds our strength." [2]

On the other hand, in his *Retractions* Augustine writes, "No one in this life can be so privileged that there should not be in his members a law fighting against the law of his mind." [3] He even includes the apostles in this indictment. Only Jesus and His mother, he says, were without sin. [4]

Why this ambivalence? For one thing, the stress of Augustine's conflict with Pelagius, who rejected any idea of original sin, drove him to a denial of the possibility of sinlessness in this life. Under the pressure of this debate Augustine developed an extreme position which contradicted views he had elsewhere advocated.

Yet there is a deeper reason for his confusion. Augustine's developed doctrine of Original Sin, while its roots lie clearly in Scripture, shows unmistakable evidence of Greek influences which distorted the biblical teaching. The result is a doctrine in which two entirely different ideas of sin become intermingled and confused.

For Augustine, the Fall introduced lust or concupiscence, which he described most vividly as sex desire. If what James calls "lust" (Jas. 1:14-15) is Original Sin or Depravity, then obviously entire sanctification is a delusion.

It is our contention, however, that such an understanding of Original Sin betrays a Hellenistic tendency to think of the physical body as sinful *per se,* an idea alien to scriptural teaching. On these premises temptation itself presupposes sin. Any doctrine of salvation which links sin so closely to the desires of the body must hesitate with Augustine to admit the possibility of heart holiness until death.

We therefore see the importance of Augustine for a study of Christian perfection. The issues raised by his theology still becloud the doctrine of salvation. The Augustinian doctrine of Original Sin has bequeathed to the Church the so-called "two-nature theory," the teaching that by grace we are given a new nature which is holy and righteous, an adventitious addition to

---

2. John L. Peters, *Christian Perfection and American Methodism* (New York and Nashville: Abingdon Press, 1946), pp. 198-99.

3. *Retractions*, 1:19.

4. *De natura et gratia*, 41-42.

the remaining old nature. The born-again believer thus has two natures, a new sinless nature and an old corrupt nature. These two natures coexist until death. Sanctification is therefore only a gradual process, awaiting death for its completion.

Unless this problem is unraveled, a biblical doctrine of perfection is impossible. No one who is serious in his desire to think clearly on the subject can sidestep the questions Augustine raises by his concept of Original Sin.

A. Augustine's Place in the Church

It would be totally unfair to Augustine, however, to limit our evaluation of his theology to these negative aspects of his teaching with respect to original sin. As both saint and theologian he stands in the lineage of Paul, Luther, Calvin, and Wesley. The secret of much of his influence lies in his mystical piety.

Augustine's love for God breathes in all that he wrote, but it is in the remarkable *Confessions* that it finds its fullest expression. No other similar spiritual autobiography was written in the Ancient Church, and it still remains perhaps the finest classic of Christian experience. On its opening page we find the key to Augustine's positive doctrine of Christian Perfection: "Thou madest us for Thyself, and our souls are restless till they repose in Thee." Here is his doctrine of the *Summum Bonum:* man's true end—his highest joy and supreme fulfillment—is in God.

"It is good, then, for me to cleave unto God, for if I remain not in Him, neither shall I in myself; but He, remaining in Himself, reneweth all things. And Thou art the Lord my God, since Thou standest not in need of my goodness" (7:11). "I sought a way of acquiring strength sufficient to enjoy Thee; but I found it not until I embraced that 'Mediator between God and man, the man Christ Jesus,' 'who is over all, God blessed forever,' calling me" (7:18). "My whole hope is only in Thy exceeding great mercy. Give what Thou commandest, and command what Thou wilt" (10:29). "I will love Thee, O Lord, and thank Thee, and confess Thy name, because Thou hast put away from me these so wicked and nefarious acts of mine. To Thy grace I attribute it, and to Thy mercy, that Thou hast melted away my sin as it were ice" (2:7). Walker observes, "Here is the deepest note of personal devotion that the church had heard since Paul, and the conception of religion as a vital relationship to the living God

65

was one the influence of which was to be permanent, even if often but partially comprehended."[5]

B. Augustine's Doctrine of Perfection

An examination of Augustine's theology reveals that it is essentially perfectionist. Its leading idea is the *Summum Bonum,* which may in some degree be enjoyed and realized in this life.

And what is the *Summum Bonum,* man's final blessedness? It is God. Our souls are restless till they find their repose in Him. In God, and in Him alone, is man's true fulfillment found.

In God man's mind finds its goal and completion. Recalling how he himself had been led to Christ through the study of philosophy and a love of truth, he says, "The inner admonition which so works upon us that we remember God, search for Him, thirst for Him (all aversion gone), comes to us from the very source of truth." At the very center of Augustine's thought is the conviction that to know God in a communion which is conscious, is the crown and goal and life. In a letter he speaks of those who have a merely intellectual love of God without having God dwelling within them, and of those in whom God dwells without their knowing it. "But most blessed are they with whom God dwells and who know it. It is this knowledge that is the fullest, truest, happiest."[6]

But Augustine knew the ethical problem which besets sinful man. While created for the knowledge of God, man has fallen away from God and is now the hapless slave of sin. Before he can love and serve God his enslaved will must be liberated. This is possible only by God's grace in Christ. Then, and only then, can man enjoy the knowledge of God which is salvation. For Augustine, therefore, Christian liberty means freedom from sin for the knowledge and service of God.

The *Summum Bonum,* therefore, is to enjoy the God who writes His Law on the tables of our hearts, by whose Presence is shed abroad in our hearts the love of God which is the fulfill-

---

5. Williston Walker, *A History of the Christian Church* (New York: Chas. Scribner's Sons, 1944), p. 179.

6. *Epistolae,* 187:21.

ment of the Law. This is the liberty promised by the gospel of Christ.

> What is better than this blessing, what happier than this happiness,—to live to God, to live on God, with whom is the fountain of life, and in whose light we shall see light. Of this life the Lord Himself speaks in these words: *This is life eternal, that they may know Thee, the only true God, and Jesus Christ whom Thou hast sent . . . We shall be like Him. . . .* This likeness begins even now to be recast in us, while the inward man is being renewed from day to day, according to the image of Him that created him.[7]

By the same token, "it is the especial wretchedness of man not to be with Him, without whom he cannot be. For beyond a doubt he is not without Him in whom he is; and yet if he does not remember, and understand, and love Him, he is not with Him."[8]

This wretchedness is the result of sin, and this barrier to "participation in the Word" is removed by the love of God shed abroad in the heart by God's Spirit. Love, therefore, is an essential element of the *Summum Bonum.* The knowledge of God and the love of God are essentially linked together in Augustine's conception of the highest good. "This love, inspired by the Holy Spirit, leads to the Son, that is to the wisdom of God, by which the Father Himself is known. . . . It is love that asks, love that seeks, love that knocks, love that reveals, love, too, that gives continuance in that which is revealed."[9]

Moreover, this love, which is the *Summum Bonum,* is thoroughly social.

> You love yourself in a way that leads to salvation when you love God better than yourself. What then you aim at in yourself you must aim at in your neighbour, namely that he may love God with a perfect affection. For you do not love him as yourself unless you try to draw him to that good which you are yourself pursuing. . . . From this commandment are born the duties of human society.[10]

In the closing pages of his masterpiece, the *City of God,* this social love of God is stressed. "How could the city of God take a beginning or be developed, or attain its proper destiny— if the life of the saints were not a social life?"[11]

---

7. *De spir. et lit.,* 22.
8. *De Trinita,* xiv:12.
9. *De mor. eccl. cath.,* 31.
10. *Ibid.,* 49.
11. *De civ. Dei,* xix:5.

Even in the life beyond there are grades and diversities, but there is no envy, no unrest, because God "shall be the end of our desires, Who shall be seen without end, loved without satiety, praised without weariness. This outgoing affection, this employment, shall certainly be, like eternal life itself, common to all."[12]

Is this perfection possible for mortal men? In his earlier treatise on the Sermon on the Mount, Augustine defined the peacemakers who are called the children of God, as those who enjoyed that peace within themselves, in whose souls all things were harmonious. The passions are subject to reason. That which is highest in man—his mind and reason—rules without resistance over his body with its desires. Reason itself is subject to the Truth, the only begotten Son of God. This is the peace enjoyed on earth by men of goodwill. "These promises can be fulfilled in this life, just as we believe them to have been fulfilled in the case of the apostles."[13]

But, as we have suggested, after his debate with Pelagius, he retracted this position.

> We do not think that the Apostles on this earth were exempt from the struggle of the flesh against the Spirit. But we believe that those promises can be fulfilled here just as they were fulfilled, according to our belief, in the Apostles, that is to say in the measure of human perfection in which perfection is possible in this life. . . . The measure is that of the perfection of which this life is capable, and not as those promises are to be fulfilled in that day of perfect peace when it shall be said: *Ubi est mors contentio tua?*[14]

There is, then, a *relative* perfection in this life. Through Christ and the inpouring of God's love by the Holy Spirit we may enjoy the knowledge of God and experience a transforming communion with Him, being gradually changed into the likeness of Him who is the Image of God. But because lust still attaches to our flesh, complete freedom from sin is impossible. "No one in this life can be so privileged that there should not be in his members a law fighting against the law of his mind." The conflict of Romans 7 remains the highest stage of Christian experience.

---

12. *Ibid.,* xxii:30.
13. *De serm. Dom. in monte,* i:4. 12.
14. *Retractions,* i:19 (Latin, "O death, where is thy sting?").

C. Evaluation

The fatal flaw in Augustine's teaching of perfection is his too easy identification of original sin with sexual lust. "There are many and various lusts, of which some have names of their own, while others have not," he writes in the *City of God.* "Yet when no object is specified, the word usually suggests to the mind the lustful excitement of the organs of generation."[15]

Although created male and female under God's command to populate the earth, Adam and Eve did not know in their unfallen state the excitement of sexual desire. Had they remained in the sinless state, "the man would have sown the seed, and the woman received it, as need required, the generative organs being moved by the will and not excited by lust."[16]

Augustine was biblical in teaching that pride, or *hybris* ("the craving for undue exaltation") was "the beginning of sin." That is, sin is essentially a perverted relationship to God in which the selfish ego usurps the throne of life. But Augustine taught that lust, which he tended to identify with physical passion, was the penal consequence of original sin. The mark of our fallen humanity is the passion which is at war with reason. This is how he understood the conflict of Romans 7, as "the quarrel between will and lust."[17] Since this quarrel continues in the lives of the noblest saints until in death they lay aside "the body of sin and death," complete sanctification is impossible in this life. Carnality is constituent to our fallen humanity, and it can be healed only by the resurrection.

This tendency to equate sin with carnal desire springs from the pagan idea that materiality is evil *per se.* It is part of Augustine's pre-Christian philosophy which was never overcome. The notion that the physical world is essentially evil was widespread in ancient times. It not only encouraged the ideal of virginity and celibacy as the true expression of perfection, it also needlessly darkened the doctrine of Original Sin. The church has found it almost impossible to rid itself of the feeling that carnality is virtually synonymous with sexual desire.

The New Testament knows no such identification of human

---

15. *De civ. Dei,* xiv:15, 16.
16. *Ibid.,* 24.
17. *Ibid.,* 23.

nature with sin. While our bodies with their desires are surely one source of temptation (Jas. 1:15-16) and therefore must be "kept under" if we are to win the prize (1 Cor. 9:25-27; cf. Rom. 8:13), freed from sin (Rom. 6:6-7) they may be yielded to God as instruments of His righteous purposes (Rom. 6:12-13; cf. 12:1) and sanctified (1 Thess. 5:23), so that in them we may glorify God (1 Cor. 6:19-20). The members of our bodies which were once sin's tools, by God's act of redemption actually become "the members of Christ"! (1 Cor. 6:15). Such is the high New Testament view of the body.

The Augustinian position betrays a confusion between the Pauline terms body *(soma)* and flesh *(sarx)*. Bringing into his interpretation of Romans 7 the Greek view that the material part of man is inherently and irremediably evil, in contrast with the soul or spirit, Augustine interpreted the struggle of Romans 7 as conflict, familiar to Greek ethics, between man's reason and his passions. John Wesley has the support of the best modern exegetes in his insistence that the flesh *(sarx)* in Romans 7 "signifies the whole man as he is by nature,"[18] not sensuality *per se*. Rather than being "the quarrel between will and lust," the struggle of Romans 7 is the frustrated existence of anyone who tries to fulfill the demands of God's law without knowing the power of Christ.

The key to Romans 7 is the phrase *autos ego* in verse 25. "*Autos ego,* 'left to myself,' says Paul, I am divided and powerless: 'With the mind I serve the law of God; but with the flesh the law of sin.'"[19] Life in the flesh as dramatically portrayed in Romans 7 is not meant to depict the Christian existence; it is life under the law. The Christian who is still fighting the battle of Romans 7 is doing so because he has fallen back under the law by trusting his own moral resources rather than the inexhaustible riches of God's grace in Christ. Having begun in the Spirit, he is trying to attain perfection by his own efforts (cf. Gal. 3:1-3).[20]

---

18. John Wesley, *Explanatory Notes upon the New Testament* (London: The Epworth Press, n.d.), p. 545.

19. J. A. T. Robinson, *The Body, a Study in Pauline Theology* (London: SCM Press, n.d.), p. 32.

20. "As Bultmann rightly stresses (*Theology of the New Testament,* 1:235 ff.), 'the mind of the flesh' stands primarily for a denial of man's depen-

As a man in Christ, of course, "I know that in me (that is, in my flesh,) dwelleth no good thing" (Rom. 7:18). But through Christ I may receive the quickening and sanctifying Spirit, and to me God may say, "You are not in the flesh, you are in the Spirit, if the Spirit of God really dwells in you" (Rom. 8:9, RSV). The final stage of Christian experience is not the conflict of Romans 7, but the freedom and victory of Romans 8. In denying the realizability of such deliverance from sin, Augustine denies both Paul's gospel and the implications of his own doctrine of Christian liberty through grace.

---

dence on God and for a trust in what is of human effort or origin. Thus, when Paul asks the Galatians, 'having begun in the Spirit, are ye now perfected in the flesh?' (Gal. 3:3), he refers, not to a lapse into sensuality, but to a return to a reliance upon the law. The flesh is concerned with serving 'the letter' (Rom. 7:6; 2:28 f.), which is 'of men' (Rom. 2:29) and represents human self-sufficiency (2 Cor. 3:5 f.)" (Robinson, *ibid.*, p. 25).

CHAPTER 7

Roman Catholic
Teaching

Augustine's idea of perfection, with differences only in detail, dominated the thought of the Western church through the Middle Ages. It is therefore unnecessary to review the many mystical writers of this long period. Two names, however, should be mentioned—Dionysius the Areopagite and Bernard of Clairvaux.

With Augustine, Dionysius believed that man's perfection consists in being united with God. But for this Christian Neoplatonist, God is the Abyss, and to be perfected, one must be plunged into "the Darkness of Unknowing" beyond all understanding. The victory of philosophy over revelation could hardly be more complete. "Yet," as Flew says, "owing to the discipleship of Johannes Scotus Erigena and through the commentaries of Hugo of St. Victor, of Thomas Aquinas, of Albertus Magnus, his writing came to a position of extraordinary influence, and his authority is quoted by medieval writers as decisive."[1]

---

1. Flew, *Idea of Perfection*, p. 219.

In Bernard of Clairvaux a warmer, more personal note of evangelical piety is introduced into Catholic devotion. In his writings, particularly in his commentary on the Song of Songs, Jesus himself returns to the center of Christian worship. In his commentary on the Song of Solomon, he says:

> When I name Jesus I set before my mind a man meek and lowly of heart, kind and collected, chaste and pitiful, conspicuous for all goodness and sanctity, and that very same Man I see as God omnipotent Who shall heal me by His example and strengthen me by His aid.[2]

The imitation of Christ becomes for Bernard the essence of devotion. While His wisdom teaches us and His love moves us, we know He is near. But above all, it is His humility we are to emulate.

We are disappointed, however, to find that when Bernard describes the highest levels of Christian attainment in this life he deserts the incarnate Lord.

> The love of the heart is in a certain sense carnal, in that it chiefly moves the heart of man towards the flesh of Christ, and what Christ in the flesh did and said. The sacred image of the God-Man, either being born or suckled or teaching or dying or rising again, is present to one in prayer, and must needs stir up the soul to the love of virtue. . . . But although such devotion to the flesh of Christ is a gift, a great gift of the Holy Ghost, nevertheless I call it carnal in comparison with that love which does not regard the Word which is Flesh, as the Word which is Wisdom, Justice, Truth, Holiness.[3]

In another book, Bernard declares that the highest kind of love cannot be attained in this life. He has outlined four degrees of love. The first is the natural love one has for himself. The second is the love of God for His bestowed benefits. The third is the love of God for His own goodness, without excluding the thought of His goodness to us.

> At this third degree one remains a long time. I do not know whether any man has arrived perfectly at the fourth stage when one only loves oneself for the sake of God. If there are any who have experienced it, let them speak; for myself, I confess, it appears to me impossible.[4]

Surely something is wrong with an ideal so defective, where

---

2. *In cant. S.*, 15.6.
3. *Ibid.*, 20.6, 8.
4. *Ibid.*, 9.7-8.

perfect love can never be reached, not even for a single moment, by the grace of God. Nevertheless, the strong strain of devotion to Jesus found in his commentary on the Song of Songs has given to Bernard a permanent place in the devotional literature of the church.

A. Thomas Aquinas

Thomas Aquinas (1225?-74) has been called "The Angelic Doctor" of the church. "In the Roman communion his influence has never ceased," Walker notes. "By declaration of Pope Leo XII, in 1879, his work is the basis of present theological instruction."[5]

Of all theologians Aquinas is most dominated by the thought of the ultimate perfection of man. One of his basic convictions is that the very nature and constitution of man contains an implicit promise of his true end, the vision and enjoyment of God. As originally created, man had, in addition to his natural powers, a superadded gift which enabled him to seek that highest good and to practice the virtues of faith, hope, and love. By sin Adam lost the gift of divine grace and corrupted his natural powers.

Man retains the power to practice the natural virtues—prudence, justice, courage, and self-control; but these, though bringing a certain degree of happiness, are not sufficient to enable one to attain his true end, the vision of God. Only free, unmerited grace can restore man to God's favor and enable him to practice the Christian virtues. No act of man can win this grace; but once redeemed, man has the power by divine grace to fulfill not only God's precepts but also the counsels of the gospel to perfection. By this grace he may enjoy perfect love now and experience the Beatific Vision of God in the life to come.

Such is the broad outline of Aquinas's doctrine. The discussion which follows is indebted to R. Newton Flew's magnificent analysis of Aquinas's teaching of perfection.[6] Dr. Flew summarizes Aquinas's view under four heads: (1) The contemplative life is superior to the active life; (2) Christian perfection consists

---

5. Walker, *History of the Christian Church,* p. 270. cf. Leo XIII, "Aeterni Patris" (Encyclical, 4 August, 1879).

6. *Idea of Perfection,* pp. 230-43.

in love, and may be attained in this life; (3) God must be loved for His own sake; and (4) Final perfection can be attained only in the life beyond.

1. *A Life of Contemplation Is Superior to the Active Life*

In order to grasp Aquinas's thought here we must appreciate fully the saying of Jesus, "Mary hath chosen that good part" (Luke 10:42). Without such sympathy, there can be no appreciation either of Roman Catholicism or of Aquinas. The saints of all communions draw upon prayer, their inward communion with God, as the source of their strength. Moreover, while this world is passing away, the life of communion knows no death. These common Christian presuppositions underlie Aquinas's position.

Yet it would be unfair to say that he disparages the active life. Great are the merits of the active life, he says, quoting Gregory. All the moral virtues pertain to the active life. By such actions we do good to our neighbor and show something of divine love. Without this love, therefore, we cannot have perfection. The active life is in some measure essential to the attainment of perfect love.

The active life of love and the contemplative life of prayer are complementary in another sense. In teaching and preaching especially, Aquinas notes, active work flows out of the fullness of contemplation as a river from the lake which is its source. There is thus a double movement in the perfect life as it is lived on earth. "The mind ascends to contemplation and then passes back to the active life to communicate the fruit of the knowledge of God."[7]

Nevertheless, the contemplative life is higher than the active. It is in knowing and loving that one reaches out to God and thereby experiences true fulfillment.

In one of his most moving articles in the *Summa Theologica,* Aquinas asks whether there is delight in contemplation. He answers that there is such delight in two ways. First, there is delight in the act of contemplation itself, for as rational creatures we were made to delight in the knowledge of the Truth. Secondly, there is delight in the contemplative life, not only by reason of the contemplation itself, but also by reason of the

---

7. *Ibid.,* p. 232.

vision of Divine Love which contemplation brings. When we see the One we supremely love, we are set aflame to love Him more. "This is the ulimate perfection of the contemplative life, that the Divine truth be not only seen but also loved."

2. Christian Perfection Consists in Love

In Question 184 of the *Summa*, Aquinas proceeds to say that the perfection of the Christian life consists chiefly in love. By active love of neighbor we express the perfection which is possible in this life; but in its Godward movement it is love which unites us to God, who is our chief end. In his doctrine of the State of Perfection he points out that there are three stages of the spiritual life, culminating in the state of perfection to which the lower stages are directed. Man's final perfection is the eternal contemplation of God, which is the ultimate fruition of love.

Love is the bond of perfection (Col. 3:14), since it binds the other virtues together in perfect unity. This love is not natural; it is the gift of God. *Caritas* (Aquinas's word) means love for God and for one's neighbors in God. It is primarily and specifically God's own love, which He communicates to man by the infusion of the Holy Spirit. The Spirit who indwells the Christian community is the Spirit whereby the Father loves the Son and the Son the Father.

Is perfect love possible in this life? In answering this question Aquinas appeals to the precept of Jesus: "You, therefore, must be perfect, as your heavenly Father who is in heaven is perfect" (Matt. 5:48, RSV). The Divine Law, he says, does not prescribe the impossible.

But what does the word perfection mean? Aquinas's answer takes into account the twofold meaning of the Greek word *(teleios)* used in the New Testament: (1) completeness, or a totality from which nothing is lacking, and (2) "fitness to purpose," or "the conformity of a thing to its end."

With respect to the first meaning, only God is absolutely perfect. But Aquinas speaks of a human perfection in which the soul loves God as much as it possibly can. Nothing is lacking to the love that can ever be there. Since the possibilities of the soul cannot be fully developed in this life, this kind of perfection is not for us as long as we are on the way. We shall have this only in heaven.

76

The third perfection refers to the removal of obstacles to the movement of love towards God. . . . Such perfection may be had in this life, and in two ways. First by the removal from man's affections of all that is contrary to love, such as mortal sin; and there can be no love apart from this perfection, and therefore it is necessary to salvation. Secondly, by the removal from man's affections, not only of whatever is contrary to love, but also of whatever hinders the mind's affections from tending wholly to God. Love is possible apart from this perfection, for instance in those who are beginners and in those who are proficient.

This third perfection is a matter of "fitness to purpose," the conformity of man to God his true end. The article above is quoted from the *Summa* (Question 184, a. 2).

However, in *De perfectione* Aquinas gives a more popular exposition of his idea of perfection. In this work he makes the same distinction between the perfection which is necessary to salvation (love excluding mortal sin) and perfect love (directing all our affections, understandings, words, and works to God) which is possible for all and incumbent upon all of us as Christians.

3. God Must Be Loved for His Own Sake

We must make a distinction between perfect and imperfect love. Perfect love for another is love for the sake of the other alone. But one may love the other partly for the benefit it brings to himself. This is imperfect love. The true love of God *(caritas)* is perfect love, which adheres to God for His own sake. The other kind of love has more of the element of hope in it. Such love that springs from hope betrays an element of self-interest and is therefore imperfect.

But how can man love God with a disinterested love? Caietan answers in a way Aquinas would have approved. A distinction is possible in the meaning of the good we can will God to have; it may mean "the good that is in Him" *or* "the good that is simply referred to God." "The good that is *in* God in His Life, His Wisdom, His Righteousness, His Mercy."[8] In the strictest sense this is God himself, and we can by love will Him to have that good *when we delight in the fact that God is what He is.* We love God with pure love when we love Him as the God He

---

8. *Ibid.*, p. 239.

has revealed himself to be, when we love Him as He is in himself.

The good that we *refer* to God is His Kingdom, the obedience due Him (Matt. 6:10). This good we will to Him when we subject ourselves fully to His will and purpose, when (in Luther's expression) *we let God be God.* This is the love of the First Commandment (Matt. 22:37-38).

This is perfect love, according to Aquinas. It is "the most excellent of the virtues" because more than Faith or Hope it attains to God. Faith looks to God and Hope yearns for God. But "Love attains God himself that it may abide in Him, and not that something may accrue to us from Him." Because Love implies an abiding in God, it is more immediate than Faith or Hope in the attainment of its end.

In this commentary on the text, "He that abideth in love abideth in God, and God in him" (1 John 4:16), Aquinas makes it clear that a pure or disinterested love is possible here and now. God is to be enjoyed. Therefore God is to be loved for himself. He may be loved immediately, and other things may be loved through God. Although no creature can love God infinitely, because all creatures are finite, God may be loved wholly according to our finite powers through the gift of His Spirit.

4. *Full Perfection Is in the Life Beyond*

We have already seen that the full development of the soul's powers is possible only in heaven. The finality of Scripture for Aquinas is seen in his treatment of the Beatific Vision: "We shall see him as he is" and "Now we see through a glass darkly, but then face to face." These are the promises upon which his theology depends.

God will not be seen by our bodily eyes. The distinction between the creature and the Creator is preserved in heaven. But at this point Aquinas introduces the reality of the heavenly body. The happiness of the saints will be greater after the resurrection "because their happiness will be not only in the soul, but also in the body."

> The more perfect a thing is in being, the more perfectly is it able to operate: wherefore the operation of the soul united to such a body will be more perfect than the operation of the separated soul. But the glorified body will be a body of this description, being altogether subject to the spirit. Therefore, since happiness consists in an operation, the soul's

happiness after its reunion with the body will be more perfect than before.[9]

Critique. There are three criticisms to be made of Aquinas's doctrine of Perfection.

a. Like Augustine, he betrays a Platonic devaluation of the body with its desires. His whole scheme of perfection is a disparagement of this world with its desires and struggles as a bad dream, or a mere passing shadow. With Augustine, Aquinas sees *cupiditas,* or the desires of the flesh, as somehow evil; and he says specifically, "perfection nulla cupiditas." That is, perfection means the elimination of bodily desires. "But," as Flew points out, "it is not in bodily desires that the evil of human nature consists; nor is it in the denial of them that perfection consists."[10]

b. Aquinas teaches a perfection which carries with it human merit. In *De perfectione* he attempts to prove that "that man merits more from God who acts under vow than he who is not under any such obligation."[11] This introduction of the notion of merit from God in virtue of a vow is far from his description of perfect love as a gift of the Spirit. Although Aquinas believed all human beings could attain to Christian perfection, apart from vows and orders, he held that "the religious state" constitutes a shortcut to perfection. Anyone who is wise will take the vows.

c. Aquinas's vision of heaven seems to be almost exclusively individualistic. In the *Summa* he says,

> If we speak of the happiness of this life, a happy man needs friends . . . that he may do good to them; that he may delight in seeing them do good; and again that he may be helped by them in his good work. . . .
> But if we speak of perfect happiness which will be in our heavenly Fatherland, the fellowship of friends is not essential to happiness; since man has the entire fullness of his perfection in God. But the fellowship of friends conduces to the well-being of happiness. . . .
> Perfection of charity is essential to happiness, as to the love of God, but not as to the love of our neighbour. Where-

---

9. *Summa Theologica,* III, q. 93, a. 1.
10. Flew, *Idea of Perfection,* p. 237.
11. *De perfectione,* c. xii.

fore if there were but one soul enjoying God, it would be happy, though having no neighbour to love.[12]

Dr. Flew comments, "So far as I can discover there is no passage in the *Summa Theologica* which neutralizes the anti-social affirmation of this article."[13] As he acknowledges, however, there are passages which *imply* another and a more Christian doctrine which allows for the perpetuation of human friendship and a real communion of the saints. "But the consequences of this more Christian idea seem not to have been realized by St. Thomas. We have a curious result. The ideal which he sketches as realizable in the present life is, in this one respect at least, superior to the fuller beatitude in the life beyond."[14]

B. Francois de Sales

Although Aquinas taught a perfection possible for all Christians, his ideal lent itself to the secluded life of the monastery. Those who took his teachings seriously would withdraw from the world to live a life of quiet contemplation.

Prior to the Reformation, Francis of Assisi had established "the Third Order" and had brought the ideal of holiness within the reach of those who are married and involved in the common activities of life. The implicit aim of the Friars Minor was the belief that perfection is possible for all Christians, "to awaken in Christian souls everywhere a striving after holiness and perfection, to keep the example of a direct following of Christ before the eyes of the world as a continuous living spectacle, and by self-sacrificing devotion to become all things to those who were spiritually abandoned and physically destitute."[15]

But the Reformation was needed to awaken in the Christian consciousness the awareness of the sacredness of the ordinary life. For Luther, the Christian ploughman at his task was as truly religious as the priest celebrating the sacrament at the altar. In the atmosphere of this new understanding the ideal of perfection was brought out into the open in an entirely new way.

Francois de Sales represents this new conception of perfec-

---

12. *Summa Theologica,* I, 11, 2. iv, a. 8.
13. Flew, *Idea of Perfection,* p. 243.
14. *Ibid.*
15. Werner, *Duns Scotus,* 2 (quoted by Flew, p. 258).

tion. He insisted that his task was "to instruct those who live in towns, in households, and at Court, whose circumstances oblige them to lead *outwardly* an ordinary life." He protested, "It is an error, nay rather an heresy, to wish to banish the devout life from the army, from the workshop, from the courts of princes, from the households of married folk."[16] And by "the devout life" he meant perfection.

His *Treatise on the Love of God* sets forth his doctrine and opens with a psychological discussion in which Francois distinguishes between the "two parts" of the soul.

> That is called inferior which reasons and draws conclusions, according to what it learns and experiences by the senses; and that is called superior, which reasons and draws conclusions according to an intellectual knowledge not founded upon the experience of sense, but on the discernment and judgement of the spirit. This superior part is called the spirit and mental part of the soul, as the inferior is termed commonly, sense, feeling, and human reason.[17]

Just as there were three courts in Solomon's temple, so there are three different degrees of reason in the temple of the soul. In the first "court" we reason according to the experience of our senses, in the second according to the human sciences, in the third according to faith. But there is a fourth place, the sanctuary, within the soul, corresponding to the Holy of Holies. Here the soul is not guided by the light of critical reasoning but enjoys a simple view of the understanding and simple feeling of the will and acquiesces and submits to the truth and the will of God. "In the sanctuary there were no windows to give light: in this degree of the soul there is no reasoning which illuminates."[18]

In the sanctuary both reason and faith are transcended and the soul enjoys contemplation. "Little bees are called nymphs or *schadons* until they make honey, and then they are called bees: so prayer is named Meditation until it has produced the honey of devotion, and then it is converted into Contemplation."[19]

> In these divine mysteries, which contain all others, there is food provided for *dear friends* to eat and drink well, and

---

16. *Introduction to the Devout Life*, i. c. 3.
17. *Treatise*, i, c. 11.
18. *Ibid.*, 12.
19. *Ibid.*, vi, c. 3.

for *dearest friends* to be inebriated. . . . To eat is to meditate
. . . to drink is to contemplate . . . but to be inebriated is to
contemplate so frequently and so ardently as to be quite out
of self to be wholly in God. O holy and sacred inebriation
which . . . does not alienate us from the spiritual sense but
from the corporal senses; does not dull or besot us, but
angelicizes and in a sort deifies us.[20]

Francois is here opening up the delights of contemplation
to the rank and file of Christian believers. What was once the
exclusive privilege of the great Contemplatives is now possible
for those engaged in "the lawful occupations" of the workaday
world. He is concerned to awaken within all men an awareness
of the divine Voice in their souls.

As soon as man thinks with even a little attention to the
divinity, he feels a certain delightful emotion of the heart,
which testifies that God is God of the human heart . . . so
that when startled by calamity, forthwith he turns to the
Divine, confessing that when all else is evil, It alone is good
towards him. . . . This pleasure, this confidence which the
human heart has naturally in God can assuredly proceed
from naught save correspondence existing between Divine
goodness and our souls; a correspondence absolute but secret,
of which everyone is aware, but which few comprehend.[21]

This is an ideal of spirituality at once mystical and humanistic. Francois de Sales reflects both Neoplatonic mysticism and
Renaissance humanism. Although he quotes St. Teresa, the
missing note is "that steady devotion to the Person of Christ,
and to Him alone, which gives the Spaniards, in spite of themselves, a sort of kinship with evangelical Christianity."[22] Nevertheless, his writings sparkle with Christian insights. "Doubtless
we are His; you have all you need."[23] "I leave you the spirit of
liberty . . . the liberty of children beloved. It is the setting free of
the Christian heart from all things, to follow the will of God once
made known."[24]

On the third centenary of Francois de Sales, Pope Pius XI
issued an encyclical in which he paid tribute to the former's
broadening of the horizons of Christian perfection.

---

20. *Ibid.*
21. *Ibid.*, i, c. 15.
22. Inge, *Christian Mysticism,* p. 231 (quoted by Flew, p. 260).
23. *Oeuvres,* xii. 385.
24. *Ibid.*, 359, 363.

Christ constituted the Church holy and the source of holiness, and all those who take her for guide and teacher must, according to the divine will, aim at holiness of life: "This is the will of God," says St. Paul, "your sanctification." What type of sanctity is meant? Our Lord himself explains it in the following manner: "Be ye perfect as your heavenly Father is perfect." Let no one think that this invitation is addressed to a small, very select number and that all others are permitted to remain in a lower degree of virtue. As is evident, this law obliges absolutely everybody without exception. Moreover, all who reach the summit of Christian perfection, and their name is legion, of every age and class, according to the testimony of history, have experienced the same weaknesses of nature and have known the same dangers. St. Augustine puts the matter clearly when he says: "God does not command the impossible, but in giving the commandment, He admonishes us to accomplish what we can according to our strength, and to ask aid to accomplish whatever exceeds our strength."[25]

As Pius says, the number of those who have found the gift of Christian perfection is legion. And Roman Catholic saints who have written on this subject are so numerous that one could write an entire book on their works. Immediately we think of the French and Spanish mystics, Juan de Castaniza, Thomas à Kempis, Molinos, Madame Guyon, and Francois Fenelon. This treatment of the Roman view of perfection will conclude with a brief sketch of Fenelon's teachings on the subject.

C. Francois Fenelon

The influence of the Protestant Reformation on the Roman idea of perfection is strongly apparent in Fenelon's thought. As chaplain in the court of Louis XIV, Fenelon was director of a small group of earnest persons who sought to live the life of deep and true spirituality in the midst of the profligate and difficult circumstances of the French court. His *Instructions et Avis sur Divers Points de la Morale et de la Perfection Chrétienne* is a devotional classic which has been translated into English under the title of *Christian Perfection*.

Evangelical warmth pervades Fenelon's writings. While he has much to say about mortification, he prescribes no morbid self-introspection. From beginning to end, perfection is the work

---

25. Peters, *Christian Perfection and American Methodism*, pp. 198-99.

of God's grace. And the detachment which marks the saint is not withdrawal from the world but inner detachment from a selfish will. Moreover, so far from being a solitary life of intellectual contemplation, the perfect life is carefree and Christlike in loving fellowship with others. Few writers have caught so fully the spirit of Jesus.

> O, how simple and serene piety can be! How likeable, discrete and sure all its proceedings! One lives much as other people do, without affectation, without any show of austerity, in an easy and sociable way, but continually bound by one's duties, but with an unrelenting renunciation of all which does not moment by moment enter into God's plans, in short with a pure vision of God to which one sacrifices the irregular impulses of human nature.[26]

Passages such as this abound in Fenelon. The perfect Christian is "free, gay, simple, a child." He does not strain after "far-fetched mortifications."[27] He accepts the providences of life with joyful resignation, and his own human frailties as opportunities for spiritual improvement. The holy life is a healthy, robust life of love.

For Fenelon, then, Christian perfection means perfect love. God cannot be satisfied with a divided heart, or a life of mere lip service. He is concerned about "what is real in our affections."

> He is a jealous God, who wants no reservations. All is not too much for him. He commands us to love him, and explains it thus: "Thou shalt love the Lord thy God, with all thy heart, with all thy soul, with all thy strength, and with all thy mind." We cannot, after that, believe that he is satisfied with a religion of only ceremony. If we do not give him everything, he wants nothing.[28]

This demand of God for single-mindedness touches the most minute details of our lives. "'That's nothing,' we say. Yes, it is nothing, but a nothing which is all for you; a nothing, which you care enough for to refuse it to God; a nothing which you scorn in words so that you may have an excuse to refuse it, but, at bottom, it is a nothing which you are keeping back from God, and which will be your undoing."[29] The love of God must bring us to the point where we are entirely His. "It is this detachment from its own will in which all Christian perfection consists."[30]

---

26. Charles F. Whiston, ed., *Christian Perfection,* trans. Mildred Whitney Stillman (New York and London: Harper & Brothers Publishers, 1947), p. 9.

27. *Ibid.,* p. 21.   28. *Ibid.,* p. 31.   29. *Ibid.,* p. 36.   30. *Ibid.,* p. 33.

What God wants is "a pure intention, a sincere detachment from ourselves."[31]

Positively, the perfect life is the imitation of Jesus. "To live as he lived, to think as he thought, to conform ourselves to his image is the seal of our sanctification."[32] But Fenelon has a word of caution here. "Let us not pretend to be able to reach this state by our own strength. But . . . let us say with confidence, 'I can do all things in him who strengthens me.'"[33] He brings this chapter to a conclusion with a prayer: "I want to follow, O Jesus, the road which thou hast taken! I want to imitate thee; I only can do so by thy grace. . . . O good Jesus, who has suffered so many shames and humiliations for love of me, print respect and love of thee deeply within my heart, and make me desire their practice!"[34]

The block which lies in the way of Christian perfection is our sinful egocentricity. "The fault in us which is the source of all the others, is love of ourselves, to which we relate everything instead of relating it to God."[35] "This 'I' of the old man" is a "subtle venom" which poisons all of life. It not only leads sinners to seek satisfaction in the things of creation, it also deceives saints into seeking themselves rather than God in their religious pursuits. Thus "they soon fall back to the depths of their own selves, where they become again their all and their own gods. Everything for self or for what is related to self, and the rest of the world is nothing."

> They do not want to be ambitious, nor avaricious, nor unfair, nor treacherous, but it is not love which steadies and continues all the virtues in opposition to these vices. It is, on the contrary, a strange fear which comes unevenly, and which holds off all those vices which go with a soul devoted to itself.
>
> This is what . . . makes me so desire a piety of pure faith and of complete death, which takes the soul away from itself without any hope of returning. . . . It is love mixed with self-love which infects us.[36]

The method God uses, therefore, in sanctifying us is a probing attack upon our egocentricity. In a passage of great depth Fenelon describes this process.

---

31. *Ibid.*, pp. 34-35.
32. *Ibid.*, p. 43.
33. *Ibid.*, p. 44.
34. *Ibid.*
35. *Ibid.*, p. 51.
36. *Ibid.*, pp. 58-59.

In the beginning, God attacked us from without. He snatched away little by little the creatures which we loved the most, contrary to his law. But this work from without, although essential to lay the foundation of the whole building, is only a very small part of it. O, but the work within, though invisible, is incomparably greater, more difficult and more wonderful! There comes a time when God, after having thoroughly despoiled us, thoroughly mortified us from without through the creatures which we set store by, attacks us from within by taking us away from ourselves. It is no longer extraneous things of which he deprives us. *This time he takes away the ego which was the centre of our love.* We only loved the rest because of this ego, and it is this ego which God pursues pitilessly and relentlessly. . . . Cut the branches of a tree and, far from making it die, you strengthen its vitality. It shoots up again on all sides. But attack the trunk, or destroy the roots, and it drops its leaves, sickens, dies. It is thus that God pleases to make us die.[37]

In the moment of self-revelation the self sees its self-idolatrous nature.

It is horrified by what it sees. It remains faithful, but it no longer sees its faithfulness. Every fault which it has had up to then, raises itself against it, and often new ones appear which it had never suspected. It finds no longer that resource of fervour and courage which sustained it before. It falls in exhaustion. It is, like Jesus Christ, sad unto death. All that is left to it is the desire to cling to nothing, and to let God act without reservation.[38]

Thus, in the moment of inward sanctification we "let God act without reservation." Fenelon insists that those who deny the possibility of perfect love in this life "do not count enough on the doctor within, who is the Holy Spirit, and who effects everything within us. . . . We act as though we were alone in this inner sanctuary. And on the contrary, God is there more intimately than we are ourselves."[39]

If anyone imagines that this perfect love is impossible and visionary, and that it is a foolish subtlety which can become a source of illusion, I have only two words with which to answer him. Nothing is impossible to God. He himself calls himself the jealous God. He only keeps us in the pilgrimage of this life to lead us to perfection. To treat this

---

37. *Ibid.,* p. 160, (italics added).
38. *Ibid.,* p. 161.
39. *Ibid.,* p. 155.

love as a visionary and dangerous subtlety is to accuse of illusion the greatest saints of every age, who have admitted this love, and who have reached through it the highest degree of spiritual life.[40]

At the heart of the Christian life, therefore, is an act of divine purification which elevates the soul to a supreme love of God. This crisis is not only preceded by the divine process of mortification, it is followed by a watchful walk before God. "The chief resource of our perfection is enclosed in that word which God said long ago to Abraham, 'Walk in my presence, and you will be perfect.'"[41] The life of true holiness is a life of watchfulness "without being too much preoccupied. . . . We never watch over ourselves as well as when we walk with God present before our eyes." The ideal is "a simple, affectionate, serene and detached vigilance."[42]

Fenelon acknowledges freely that the perfect life is not inconsistent with distractions and periods of spiritual dryness. If the enlightened saint is not thrown into despair by his remaining imperfections, neither is he by the emotional depressions which occasionally come. Fenelon explains, "Pure love is only singleness of will. . . . It is a love which loves without feeling, a pure faith which believes without seeing. So the love is chaste because it is God in himself and for himself" we are commanded and enabled to love.[43]

> It even often happens that we go a long time without thinking that we love him, and we love him no less during this period than in those in which we make him the most tender protestations. True love rests in the depths of the heart.[44]
>
> As for involuntary distractions, they do not disturb love at all, since it exists in the will, and the will never has distractions when it does not want to have them. When we notice them, we let them fall, and we turn again to God. Thus, while the outer senses of the bride are slumbering, her heart watches, her love does not relax. A tender father does not always think distinctly of his son. A thousand objects take away his imagination and his mind. But these distractions never interrupt the paternal love. Whenever his son returns to his mind, he loves him, and he feels in the depths

---

40. *Ibid.*, p. 41.
41. *Ibid.*, p. 27.
42. *Ibid.*, p. 23.

43. *Ibid.*, p. 53.
44. *Ibid.*, p. 18.

of his heart that he has not stopped loving him for a single moment, although he has stopped thinking about him. Such should be the love for our heavenly Father, a simple love, without suspicion and without uneasiness.[45]

In all His ministrations, God has only one purpose in mind —to wean us away from ourselves and to bind us to His love. "It is for God to increase, when it pleases him, this ability to keep the experience of his presence."[46]

Indeed, we must remind ourselves again of Jesus Christ, whom his Father abandoned on the cross. God withdrew all feeling and all reflection to hide himself from Jesus Christ. That was the last blow from the hand of God which smote the man of sorrows. That was the consummation of his sacrifice. We never so need to abandon ourselves to God as when he seems to abandon us.

So let us take light and consolation when he gives them, but without becoming attached to them. When he plunges us into the night of pure faith, then let us go into this night, and let us lovingly suffer this agony. . . . We accept all, even the trials by which we are tested. Thus we are secretly in peace because of his will, which keeps reserve strength in the depths of its soul to endure the war. Blessed be God, who has done such things in us in spite of our unworthiness![47]

---

45. *Ibid.*, p. 55.
46. *Ibid.*
47. *Ibid.*, p. 56.

CHAPTER 8

Reformation Theology

The most decisive contribution of the Reformation to the idea of Christian perfection was the recovery of the New Testament teaching that the full Christian life can be lived in any of the ordinary callings. The Augsburg Confession expresses this truth in its article on the subject:

> Christian perfection is this, to fear God sincerely, and again to conceive great faith, and to trust that for Christ's sake God is pacified towards us; to ask, and with certainty to look for help from God in all our affairs, according to our calling; and meantime outwardly to do good works diligently and to attend to our calling. In these things doth consist true perfection and the true worship of God; it doth not consist in celibacy, or mendicancy, or in vile apparel.[1]

Speaking of the work of the maid who cooks and cleans and does other housework, Luther says, "Because God's command is there, even such a small work must be praised as a service to

---

1. Article 27.

God, far surpassing the holiness and asceticism of all monks and nuns."[2] Such statements as these are frequent in Luther's sermons. And Melanchthon can say, "All men, in whatever vocation they are, ought to seek perfection, i.e. to increase in the fear of God, in faith, in brotherly love, and similar spiritual virtues."[3]

A. Martin Luther

The conviction of the holiness of the ordinary life of the Christian believer was a direct outgrowth of Luther's rediscovery of the gospel. For him, Jesus Christ was everything. Two New Testament truths controlled his thought—the humanity of our Lord and the centrality of His saving work.

In the first place, Luther placed the humanity of Jesus at the very center of Christian devotion. Flew rightly claims, "Apart from the Gospels and the Epistle to the Hebrews, there is nothing in Christian literature before him quite like his vividness, his profound religious feeling for the human life of Jesus Christ. It is there, in that human life, that he finds God."[4] If Bernard deserted the incarnate Lord at the higher stages of contemplation,[5] Luther could say of the New Testament Jesus:

> When I thus imagine Christ, then do I picture Him truly and properly . . . and then I let go utterly all thoughts and speculations concerning the Divine Majesty and glory, and hang and cling to the humanity of Christ . . . and I learn thus through Him to know the Father. Thus arises such a light and knowledge within me that I know certainly what God is, and what is His mind.[6]

It would be difficult to exaggerate the significance of this radical shift of focus for Christian piety which Luther effected. For medieval devotion, the highest expression of the spiritual life was the knowledge and love of God found in contemplation. For Luther the knowledge of God was not a human discovery won through contemplation, but God's own revelation and gift through Jesus Christ.

---

2. Quoted by Flew, *Idea of Perfection*, p. 251.
3. *Ibid.*, p. 252.
4. *Ibid.*, p. 248.
5. *Ibid.*
6. Hermann, *Communion with God*, E. tr. 143.

No one shall taste Deity save as He wills to be tasted; and thus He wills: to wit, that He shall be looked on in the humanity of Christ. If thou dost not find Deity thus, thou shalt never rest. Hence let them go on speculating and talking about contemplation, how everything is a wooing of God, and how we are always having a foretaste of eternal life, and how spiritual souls set about their life of contemplation. But do not thou learn to know God thus, I charge thee.[7]

Another difference between Roman and Lutheran piety should be noted. Despite its ideal of the intellectual contemplation of God, Roman piety was strongly *ethical:* Christian perfection meant perfect love—loving God for himself and neighbor in God. For Luther the *religious* experience of forgiveness of sins was the shining center of piety:

For just as the sun shines and illuminates none the less brightly when I close my eyes, so this throne of grace, or this forgiveness of sins, is always there, even although I fall. And just as I see the sun again when I open my eyes, so also I have forgiveness of sins once again when I look and come back to Christ. Wherefore we are not to measure forgiveness so narrowly as fools dream.[8]

How then does faith make us holy? First of all, all believers enjoy a "positional" or imputed perfection. A contemporary interpreter of Luther explains this view:

Because faith receives and accepts the gift of God and thus men become saints through faith, "holy" becomes the equivalent of "believing." The saints, or holy ones, are the believers, and "to make holy" means "to be made a believer." In Luther's explanation the emphasis is shifted from sanctity and sanctifying to faith and being brought to faith except that there is no real difference between the two.[9]

In this view, faith *is* perfection. This is not to say, however, that Luther ascribes to faith no sanctifying power. In the Preface to the Epistle to the Romans he explains how "faith alone makes righteous and fulfills the law."

For out of Christ's merit it brings the Spirit, and the Spirit makes the heart glad and free as the law requires that it shall be. Faith, however, is a divine work within us. It changes us and makes us to be born anew of God (John 1); it

7. *Werke* (Erlangen ed.), xxv. 334.

8. Hermann, *Communion with God,* E. tr. 249.

9. Herbert Girgensohn, *Teaching Luther's Catechism,* p. 180 (quoted by Donald Metz, *Studies in Biblical Holiness,* p. 16).

kills the old Adam and makes us altogether new and different men, in heart and spirit and mind and powers, and it brings with it the Holy Ghost. O, it is a living, busy, active, mighty thing, this faith, and so it is impossible for it not to do good works incessantly. It does not ask whether there are good works to do, but before the question rises it has already done them, and is always doing them. . . . It is impossible to separate works from faith, as impossible as to separate heat and light from fire.[10]

In his essay *On Christian Liberty*, Luther takes another approach to the question of sanctifying faith. First, the Christian virtues become the possession of the believer's soul "just as iron exposed to the fire glows like fire, on account of its union with fire." In the second place, faith honors God by ascribing to Him the glory of being faithful to His promises. In so doing the soul gives up itself to be dealt with as it may please God. "The third incomparable grace of faith is that it unites the soul to Christ, as the wife to the husband, by which mystery, as the Apostle teaches, Christ and the soul are made one flesh. Whatever belongs to Christ the soul can claim. Christ is full of grace, life, and salvation. Let faith step in, and there is the delightful prospect of redemption and victory."

Flew concludes: "Thus the believing soul, by the pledge of its faith in Christ, becomes free from all sin, fearless of death, safe from hell, and endowed with the eternal righteousness, life, and salvation of the husband Christ."[11]

Luther here comes to the very threshold of the New Testament doctrine of perfection. But because he subscribes to Augustine's doctrine of Original Sin as remaining lust or concupiscence,[12] he shrinks from asserting with Paul the possibility of a present deliverance from sin. "The remnants of sin cleave yet fast in our flesh: therefore, as touching the flesh, we are sinners, yea, after that we have received the Holy Ghost."[13] Again he

---

10. *Works of Martin Luther* (Philadelphia: Westminster Press, 1932), 6:449, 450, 451.

11. Flew, *Idea of Perfection,* p. 250.

12. In his *Commentary on Genesis,* Luther says, "But now, since the sin of the fall, all know how great is the excitement of the flesh; which is not only furious in concupiscence, but also in disgust, after it has satisfied its desire."— Hugh Thompson Kerr, *A Compend of Luther's Theology* (Philadelphia: Westminster Press, 1943), p. 81.

13. *Epistle Sermon, Pentecost Sunday* (Kerr, *Compend,* p. 69).

says, "Sin is still present in all the baptised and holy men on earth, and they must fight against it."[14]

> Original sin, after regeneration, is like a wound that begins to heal; though it be a wound, yet it is in course of healing, though it still runs and is sore. So original sin remains in Christians until they die, yet itself is mortified and continually dying. Its head is crushed in pieces, so that it cannot condemn us.[15]

Luther guards himself against antinomianism. Although sin continues to be "felt" in "a truly Christian life," it must not be "favored." "Thus we are to fast, pray, labor, to subdue and suppress lust. . . . While flesh and blood continue, so long sin remains; wherefore it is ever to be struggled against."[16] The "newness of life" which we have through Christ, therefore, *"begins* only, in this life, nor ever can be perfected in this flesh."[17] Nevertheless, the Holy Spirit continues to carry forward His sanctifying work within us if we faithfully fight against sin. "Thus we are constantly to grow in sanctification and ever to become more and more 'a new creature' in Christ."[18]

Clearly it is Luther's identification of Paul's doctrine of the flesh with human nature itself which cripples his teaching of sanctification and precludes the possibility of a Lutheran doctrine of present evangelical perfection.

B. John Calvin

Of the evangelical nature of Calvin's theology there can be absolutely no question. For him "a true conversion of our life to God" consists "in the mortification of our flesh and of the old man and in the vivification of the Spirit."[19] This is effected by our participation in Christ:

> For if we truly partake of his death, our old man is crucified by its power, and the body of sin expires, so that the corruption of our former nature loses all its vigour (Romans

---

14. *An Argument in Defense of All the Articles of Dr. Martin Luther Wrongly Condemned in the Roman Bull* (Kerr, Compend, p. 86).

15. *Table-Talk,* No. CCLVI.

16. *Commentary on Peter and Jude* (Kerr, Compend, p. 114).

17. *Commentary on Genesis* (Kerr, Compend, 83; Luther's italics).

18. *On the Councils and the Churches* (Kerr, Compend, p. 133).

19. *Institutes of the Christian Religion, by John Calvin,* trans. John Allen (Philadelphia: Board of Christian Education, n.d.), 1:654.

vi. 5, 6). If we are partakers of his resurrection, we are raised by it to a newness of life, which corresponds to the righteousness of God.[20]

"Thus, therefore, the children of God are liberated by regeneration from the servitude of sin."[21] The life of the Christian is to be a life of holiness. "With what better foundation can it begin," Calvin asks, "than when [Scripture] admonishes us that we ought to be holy because *our God is holy?*" (Lev. 19:2).

> When we hear any mention of our union with God, we should remember that holiness must be the bond of it, not that we attain communion with him by the merit of holiness . . . but because it is a peculiar property of his glory not to have any intercourse with iniquity and uncleanness.[22]

Calvin, however, is very careful to disclaim that he is advocating a doctrine of Christian Perfection:

> Yet I would not insist upon it as absolutely necessary, that the manners of a Christian should breathe nothing but the perfect gospel; which, nevertheless, ought both to be wished and to be aimed at. But I do not so rigorously require evangelical perfection as not to acknowledge as a Christian one who has not yet attained to it; for then all would be excluded from the Church; since no man can be found who is not a great distance from it.[23]

The reason for Calvin's qualification of Christian holiness is not hard to discover. With Augustine and Luther he sees the believer as hopelessly trapped by the flesh. "We maintain," he insists, "that sin always exists in the saints until they are divested of the mortal body, because their flesh is the residence of that depravity of concupiscence which is repugnant to all rectitude."[24]

Quoting Augustine copiously, he bases his pessimistic position on his understanding of Romans 7, confidently asserting, "Paul there speaks of a regenerate man."[25] Indeed, this is "the conflict between the flesh and the spirit which he experienced in his own person."[26] In a passage in which he cites Plato by name he explains the Pauline doctrine of the flesh in Platonic terms: "As long as we inhabit *the prison of our body* we shall have to

---

20. *Ibid.*, p. 657.
21. *Ibid.*, p. 658.
22. *Ibid.*, pp. 746-47.
23. *Ibid.*, p. 749.

24. *Ibid.*, p. 659.
25. *Ibid.*, p. 660.
26. *Ibid.*, p. 664.

maintain an incessant conflict with the vices of our corrupt nature."[27]

With such a Platonic view of the body Calvin must dismiss the Pauline prayers for perfection in believers (quoting 1 Thess. 3:13):

> These passages, indeed, the Celestines formerly perverted in order to prove a perfection of righteousness in the present life. We think it sufficient briefly to reply, with Augustine, "that all the pious ought, indeed, to aspire to this object, to appear one day immaculate and guiltless before the presence of God; but since the highest excellency in this life is nothing more than a progress toward perfection, we shall never attain it, till, being divested at once of mortality and sin, we shall fully adhere to the Lord."
>
> Nevertheless, I shall not pertinaciously contend with any person who chooses to attribute to the saints the character of perfection, provided he also defines it in the words of Augustine himself; who says, "When we denominate the virtue of the saints perfect, to this perfection itself belongs the acknowledgement of imperfection, both in truth and in humility.[28]

Historically, Calvinism has been the avowed enemy of any doctrine of Christian Perfection. Many Calvinists, however, have embraced a doctrine of practical holiness through the infilling of the Holy Spirit. While these teachers deny the possibility of sin's destruction, they do advocate the possibility of a life of victory over the old remaining nature for those who put themselves under the direction and control of the indwelling Spirit. But as long as Christians inhabit this mortal body, they must contend with the old nature of sin. The error of this view, in our judgment, is the too easy identification of the body itself with sin. Such a position is Platonic rather than Pauline, Greek rather than Christian.

---

27. *Ibid.*, p. 672 (italics added).
28. *Ibid.*, 2:60.

CHAPTER 9

Perfection in the Post-Reformation Era

Theologically, the most significant accomplishment of the Reformers was the restoration of the doctrine of justification by faith to its rightful place of primacy. Man can do nothing of himself to accomplish his salvation. No merit attaches to any human works or righteousness; salvation is by grace alone, through faith alone, to the glory of God alone. Justification by faith is, in Luther's formula, "the article upon which the Church rises or falls."

It would be impossible, therefore, to overstate the contribution of the Reformers in recovering the fundamental scriptural doctrine of justification by faith. But, as Dr. Paul Sherer said of certain neo-Protestants of this century, "If justification was the apple of their eye, sanctification was their blind spot." In Adolph Harnack's oft quoted statement, they "neglected far too much the moral problem, the *Be ye holy, for I am holy.*"[1] In

---

1. *History of Dogma,* vii. 267 (cited by Flew, *Idea of Perfection,* p. 257).

their reaction against the works religion of medieval Catholicism, the Reformers went too far and failed to do justice to the New Testament teaching of the Spirit and His work of sanctification. The result tended to be a strong emphasis upon orthodoxy to the neglect of a healthy doctrine of holiness and Christian spirituality.

Is this why widespread spiritual revival did not accompany the Reformation? The foundation was there, to be sure, but it was left to groups like the German Pietists, the Quakers, and the Moravians to attempt the superstructure of a Spirit-filled church. It was the church's great loss that Luther and Calvin were unable to overcome their Augustinian pessimism concerning the possibilities of grace. By failing to develop a full-orbed teaching of sanctification, the Reformers left a spiritual vacuum in Protestantism.

A. Pietism

Philipp Jakob Spener (1633-1705) is regarded as the "father" of Pietism, a movement of spiritual renewal among Lutherans in Germany. Spener in turn gained his inspiration from Arndt's *Wahren Christentum,* an earlier work which stressed the necessity of the new birth and the need of combining mysticism and practical ethics. In the background of influence on the entire theology of Pietism is the "Jesus-mysticism" of Bernard of Clairvaux.[2] Spener's *Pia Desideria* sets forth the principles of the movement:

1. Exposition of Scripture by the preachers in classes
2. Laymen are a spiritual priesthood (cf. Luther)
3. Knowledge of God is of the heart, not of the head
4. Prayer for healing of schisms and for increase of love
5. Theologians to increase in piety as well as learn doctrine
6. Sermons not to defend doctrines but to edify hearers[3]

Spener's tolerance was a remarkable exception to the prevailing dogmatism of his time. His motto has become classic: "In essentials unity, in nonessentials liberty, in all things charity."

---

2. George Allen Turner, *The Vision Which Transforms* (Kansas City: Beacon Hill Press of Kansas City, 1964), p. 182.

3. *Ibid.,* p. 183.

The distinguishing mark of Pietism was the quest for personal holiness. Spener organized seekers after holiness into classes he called *collegia pietatis*. His emphasis was more upon the new birth than justification. The proof of one's justification before God, he insisted, is loving obedience and a passion for holiness. Spener stressed Christ in us more than Christ for us, and communion with God more than reconciliation to God. One who is born of God can, with a pure intention, keep God's law fully, since what God requires is not perfect knowledge but simplicity of motive. Love is thus the fulfilling of the law. Christian perfection is therefore relative, a gradual process to be completed in the next life.

Spener's successor was A. H. Franke (1663-1727), whose teaching on Christian perfection was more typically Lutheran. Sanctification was stressed, but it was "fused and confused" with justification.[4] In his work entitled *The Perfection of the Christian,* Franke describes three stages in the progress of the believer toward the final goal. In advancing toward perfection one moves from childhood to youth to spiritual manhood. The decisive mark of spiritual maturity is the ability to distinguish between good and evil (cf. Heb. 5:14).[5]

B. Quakerism

There may be some truth in Thomas Carlyle's claim that George Fox (1624-90) was "the protestant of Protestants." Flew thinks his teachings may be regarded as "the logical outcome of the Lutheran conception of faith" as man's utter trust in Christ. His doctrine of the Inner Light is not the same thing as justification by faith, but it does raise to the highest level the sense of personal responsibility enshrined in the doctrine.[6] Flew believes that in spiritual and ethical insight Fox goes far deeper than the Reformers, "and he did so precisely in virtue of his teaching on perfection." Flew then makes a very strong claim: "The Quaker doctrine has this distinction among all the types of teaching from the third century to the eighteenth, that it returned wholeheartedly to the attitude of the New Testament."[7]

From the beginning Fox taught that the Inner Light means

---

4. *Ibid.,* p. 184.
5. Flew, *Idea of Perfection,* pp. 276-77.
6. *Ibid.,* p. 281.
7. *Ibid.,* p. 282.

emancipation from sin. Not long after his religious awakening he records a second experience, which occurred in 1648, when he was 24 years of age:

> Now was I come in spirit through the Flaming Sword, into the Paradise of God. All things were new, and all creation gave another smell unto me than before, beyond what words can utter. I knew nothing but pureness and innocency and righteousness, being renewed into the image of God by Christ Jesus, so that I say I was come up to the state of Adam, which he was before he fell.[8]

Continuing his account, he reports he was "taken up in spirit to see into another and more stedfast state than Adam's in innocency, even into a state in Christ Jesus that should never fall." This was an extreme position, which was to be later modified by Quaker writers, but for Fox himself, this experience was entrance into what apparently became a state of abiding victory over sin.

In his imprisonment at Derby two years later he said to "divers professors" who "came to plead for sin and imperfection":

> If your faith be true, it will give you victory over sin and the devil, purify your hearts and consciences and bring you to please God, and give you access to Him again. But they could not endure to hear of purity, and of victory over sin and the devil: for they said they could not believe that any could be free from sin this side of the grave.[9]

The accepted doctrine of the time could not make place for a doctrine like that of Fox. English theology of all schools was dominated by the Augustinian conviction of the ineradicable sinfulness of man. Matching their pessimism was a pathetically low state of morals and spirituality in the land. It is understandable that Fox should write, after a special "opening" from the Lord: "He showed me that the priests were not of the true faith, which Christ is author of; that faith which purifies and gives victory, and brings the people to have access to God, by which they please God."[10]

After other illuminations, Fox's sense of mission was clarified:

> It was to bring them off from all the world's fellowships, and prayings, and singings, which stood in forms without

---

8. George Fox, *Journal.*   9. *Ibid.*   10. *Ibid.*

power; that their fellowship might be with the Holy Ghost, and in the Eternal Spirit of God; that they might pray in the Holy Ghost, and sing in the Spirit, and with the grace that comes from Jesus.[11]

C. E. Hinshaw observes that, in Fox's mind, "salvation is not merely exemption from the punishment due to sin, but consists in being delivered from the power and dominion of evil. . . . The righteousness of Christ is not a cloak to cover the deformity of sin, but a fountain of living waters to purify the soul."[12]

Fox's teaching that a Christian may be restored to the innocency of Adam before the Fall, "even to a state in Christ Jesus that should never fall," was of course extreme and unbiblical. The lapse of James Nayler proved to be a great embarrassment, and thereafter especially Quaker writers sought to guard Fox's teachings from fanaticism. William Penn carefully qualifies the doctrine in this way:

> Because we have urged the necessity of a perfect freedom from sin, and a thorough sanctification in body, soul, and spirit, whilst on this side of the grave, by the operation of the holy and perfect Spirit of our Lord Jesus Christ, according to the testimony of holy scripture, we are made (i.e. represented as being) so presumptuous, as to assert the fullness of perfection and happiness to be attainable in this life: whereas we are not only sensible of those human infirmities that attend us, whilst clothed with flesh and blood; but know that here we can only "know in part, and see in part": the perfection of wisdom, glory, and happiness, being reserved for another and better world.[13]

Robert Barclay became the official theologian of Quakerism. In his Eighth and Ninth Propositions he advances a balanced doctrine of Christian Perfection:

> In whom this pure and holy *birth* is fully brought forth, the body of death and sin comes to be crucified and removed, and their hearts united and subjected to the *truth;* so as not to obey any suggestions or temptations of the evil one, but to be free from actual sinning and transgressing of the *law of God,* and in that respect *perfect:* yet doth this *perfection* still admit of a growth, and there remaineth always in some part

---

11. *Ibid.*

12. Cited by Turner, *The Vision Which Transforms,* p. 180.

13. *A Testimony to the Truth of God* (cited by Flew, *Idea of Perfection,* p. 287).

a possibility of sinning, where the mind doth not most diligently and watchfully attend unto the Lord.[14]

Although this gift and inward grace of God be sufficient to work out salvation, yet in those in whom it is resisted, it both may and doth become their condemnation. Moreover, they in whose hearts it hath wrought in part to purify and sanctify them in order to their further perfection, may, by disobedience, fall from it, *turn it to wantonness, make shipwreck of faith, and after having tasted the heavenly gift, and been made partakers of the Holy Ghost, again fall away;* yet such an increase and stability in the truth may in this life be attained, from which there can be no total apostasy.[15]

The crowning glory of the Quaker doctrine was that it found its center in the cross of Christ. "There George Fox found the power for that unwearying love which is the perfect life. . . . The favourite sentence of Fox was: 'The Cross is the power of God.' The Atonement was inward."[16]

Now that ye know the power of God and are come to it— which is the Cross of Christ, that crucifies you to the state that Adam and Eve were in, in the Fall, and so to the world, by this power of God ye come to see the state they were in before they fell, which power of God is the Cross, in which stands the everlasting glory; which brings up into the righteousness, holiness, and image of God, and crucifies to the unrighteousness, unholiness, and image of Satan.[17]

Brought back to the cross of Christ, the restored James Nayler's dying words set forth the Quaker teaching in beautiful balance:

There is a spirit which I feel that delights to do no evil, nor to revenge any wrong, but delights to endure all things. . . . Its hope is to outlive all wrath and contention, and to weary out all exaltation and cruelty, or whatever is of a nature contrary to itself. It sees to the end of all temptations. As it bears no evil in itself, so it conceives none in thoughts to any other. If it be betrayed, it bears it, for its ground and spring is the mercies and forgiveness of God. Its crown is meekness, its life is everlasting love unfeigned; and takes its kingdom with entreaty and not with contention, and keeps it by lowliness of mind.[18]

---

14. Cited by Flew, *Idea of Perfection*, p. 288.
15. *Ibid.*, p. 289.
16. *Journal* (cited by Flew, *Idea of Perfection*, p. 291).
17. *Ibid.*, p. 292.
18. *Ibid.*

C. Moravianism

The Moravians, or *Unitas Fratrum* as they preferred to be called, were descendants of the Taborites, a strict branch of John Huss's disciples. In the 1720s they settled on the estate of Nicolas Ludwig, count of Zinzendorf, in Herrnhut, Germany. Here they united with another group of refugees, the Schwenckfelders, and after ironing out certain doctrinal issues adopted with them the *Ratio Disciplinae* of Comenius.

In the summer of 1727 the Herrnhut community experienced a remarkable outpouring of the Holy Spirit. This they regarded as another Pentecost and as the birthday of the revived Church. They formed themselves into small bands for spiritual edification and began immediately to send out missionaries, 50 years before Carey and the modern missionary movement.

It was a group of these missionaries who bore to John Wesley on his voyage to Georgia the first witness he had heard to salvation by faith alone. Attracted to them by their evident New Testament spirit, Wesley maintained close connections with the Moravians during his two-year ministry in America. Returning to London in 1738, he encountered another Moravian, Peter Böhler, who proved to be God's instrument to show Wesley the true nature of justifying faith. He encouraged Wesley, urging, "Preach faith *till* you have it; and then, *because* you have it, you *will* preach it."[19]

Following his advice Wesley began to preach faith. Two months later, on the evening of May 24, Wesley received his notable heartwarming experience in a society (probably Moravian) meeting on Aldersgate Street, London. "I did trust in Christ, Christ alone for salvation," Wesley notes in his *Journal;* "and an assurance was given me that he had taken away *my* sins, even *mine,* and saved *me* from the law of sin and death."[20]

Through the Moravians also, Wesley first encountered "persons saved from inward as well as outward sins." On a personal visit to Herrnhut in August of 1738, where he had gone to converse "with these living witnesses of the full power of faith," he met Arvid Gradin, who gave him the first definition of "the full assurance of faith" he had ever heard from "any living

---

19. Wesley, *Works,* 1:86.
20. *Ibid.,* p. 103.

man." This was the word Wesley had long been seeking, and he took it down word for word in Latin, which he also translated:

> Repose in the blood of Christ. A firm confidence in God, and persuasion of his favour; serene peace and steadfast tranquillity of mind, with a deliverance from every fleshly desire, and from every outward and inward sin. In a word, my heart, which before was tossed like a troubled sea, was still and quiet, and in a sweet calm.[21]

From Michael Linner, "the eldest of the church," and Christian David he first learned the distinction between a justified and fully sanctified believer. Referring to Linner's preaching, Wesley writes:

> Thrice he described the state of those who are "weak in faith," who are justified, but have not yet a new, clean heart; who have received forgiveness through the blood of Christ, but have not received the constant indwelling of the Holy Ghost. . . .
>
> A second time he . . . showed the nature of that intermediate state, which most experience between that bondage which is described in the seventh chapter of the Epistle to the Romans, and the full glorious liberty of the children of God, described in the eighth, and many other parts of scripture. . . . This he . . . explained from the scriptures which describe the state the Apostles were in . . . till the descent of the Holy Ghost at the day of Pentecost.[22]

The Moravians, however, did not stress doctrine, and it is not easy to ascertain their creed. In later doctrinal discussions with Moravians Wesley encountered a widely divergent understanding of perfection, which reflected the traditional Lutheran and Reformed emphasis.

Three years after his Aldersgate experience, in May, 1741, Wesley had "a conversation of several hours with P. Böhler and Mr. Spangenberg. One subject was a new creature. Mr. Spangenberg's account of which was:

> "The moment we are justified, a new creature is put into us. This is otherwise termed, the new man.
>
> "But notwithstanding, the old creature or the old man remains in us till the day of our death.
>
> "And in this old man there remains an old heart, corrupt and abominable. For inward corruption remains in the soul as long as the soul remains in the body.

---

21. *Ibid.*, p. 140.
22. *Ibid.*, p. 117.

"But the heart which is in the new man is clean. And the new man is stronger than the old; so that though corruption continually strives, yet while we look to Christ it cannot prevail."

I asked him, "Is there still an old man in you?" He said, "Yes; and will be as long as I live." I said, "Is there then corruption in your heart?" He replied, "In the heart of my old man there is: But not in the heart of my new man." I asked, "Does the experience of your brethren agree with yours?" He answered, "I know what I have now spoken is the experience of all the brethren and sisters throughout our Church."

A few of our [Methodist] brethren and sisters sitting by, then spoke what they had experienced. He told them, (with great emotion, his hand trembling much,) "You all deceive your souls. There is no higher state than that I have described. You are in a very dangerous error. You do not know your own hearts. You fancy your corruptions are taken away, whereas they are only covered. Inward corruption never can be taken away, till our bodies are in the dust."[23]

In September of 1741, Zinzendorf was in London and met with Wesley. The two men had a conversation on the subject of perfection, which Wesley later recorded in Latin. The following is a translation of the key passages:

Z. I acknowledge no inherent perfection in this life. This is the error of errors. I pursue it through the world with fire and sword. . . . Christ is our sole perfection. Whoever follows inherent perfection, denies Christ.

W. But I believe that the Spirit of Christ works this perfection in true Christians.

Z. By no means. All our perfection is in Christ. All Christian perfection is Faith in the blood of Christ. Our whole Christian perfection is imputed, not inherent. We are perfect in Christ, in ourselves we are never perfect.

W. I think we strive about words.

However, the real difference between Wesley and Zinzendorf becomes clear in what follows:

W. I mean nothing else by perfection than [loving God with all his heart].

Z. But this is not his holiness. He is not more holy if he loves more, or less holy if he loves less.

W. What! Does not every believer while he increases in love, increase equally in holiness?

Z. Not at all. In the moment he is justified, he is wholly sanctified. From that time he is neither more nor less holy, even unto death. . . .

---

23. *Ibid.*, p. 308.

W. Do we not, while we deny ourselves, die more and more to the world and live to God?

Z. We reject all self-denial. We trample on it. . . . No purification precedes perfect love.[24]

It was after this conversation that Wesley separated his Methodists from the Fetters Lane Society, where they had been associated with the Moravians; but to the end of his days Wesley acknowledged his debt to them, including in the "Plain Account of Christian Perfection" the testimony of Arvid Gradin, cited above, "The first account I have ever heard from any living man of what I had learned myself from the oracles of God, and had been praying for, (with the little company of my friends,) and expecting, for several years."[25]

---

24. *Ibid.*, pp. 323-25 (translated by Flew, *Idea of Perfection*, pp. 278-79).
25. Wesley, *Works*, 11:370.

CHAPTER **10**

The Wesleyan Doctrine of Perfection

"The Wesleyan reconstruction of the Christian ethic of life," George Croft Cell claims, "is an original and unique synthesis of the Protestant ethic of grace with the Catholic ethic of holiness." In Wesley's thought the distinctively religious emphasis of the early Protestant doctrine of justification by faith is reunited, as in the New Testament, with the special interest of Catholic thought and piety in the ideal of holiness and evangelical perfection.[1]

Cell argues convincingly that the "homesickness for holiness," the yearning for Christlikeness which caught the imagination of St. Francis of Assisi, constitutes "the innermost kernel of Christianity." It was precisely this "lost accent of Christianity" which fell into the background of interest in early Protestantism. Cell quotes approvingly Harnack's observation that

---

1. George Croft Cell, *The Rediscovery of John Wesley* (New York: Henry Holt and Co., 1935), p. 347.

Lutheranism, in its purely religious understanding of the gospel, neglected too much the moral problem, the *Be ye holy, for I am holy.* "Right here," Cell continues, "Wesley rises to mountain heights. He restored the neglected doctrine of holiness to its merited position in the Protestant understanding of Christianity."[2]

From the perspective of historic Christianity, therefore, the Wesleyan doctrine of Christian Perfection is no theological provincialism. In fusing justification and sanctification, original sin and Christian Perfection, it restored the New Testament message to its original wholeness. Wesley "had glimpsed the underlying unity of Christian truth in both the Catholic and Protestant traditions."[3]

Wesley understood his message in this way. In his sermon "On God's Vinyard" he says:

> It has been frequently observed, that very few were clear in their judgment both with regard to justification and sanctification. Who has wrote (sic) more ably than Martin Luther on justification by faith alone? And who was more ignorant of the doctrine of sanctification, or more confused in his conceptions of it? . . . On the other hand, how many writers of Roman Church (as Francis Sales and Juan Castiniza, in particular) have wrote strongly and scripturally on sanctification, who, nevertheless, were entirely unacquainted with the nature of justification! inasmuch as the whole body of their Divines at the Council of Trent . . . totally confound sanctification and justification together. But it has pleased God to give the Methodists a full and clear knowledge of each, and the wide difference between them.
>
> We know, indeed, that at the same time a man is justified, sanctification properly begins. For when he is justified he is "born again," "born of the Spirit;" which, although it is not (as some suppose) the whole process of sanctification, is doubtless the gate to it. Of this likewise, God has given [the Methodists] a full view. . . .
>
> They maintain, with equal zeal and diligence, the doctrine of free, full, present justification, on the one hand, and of entire sanctification both of heart and life on the other; being as tenacious of inward holiness as any Mystic, and of outward, as any Pharisee.[4]

---

2. *Ibid.*, p. 359.

3. Albert Outler, *John Wesley* (New York: Oxford University Press, 1964), p. viii.

4. Wesley, *Works*, 7:204-5.

The genius of the Wesleyan teaching, says Dr. Cell, is that it neither confounds nor divorces justification and sanctification but places "equal stress upon the one and the other."

A. The Wesleyan Formulation

Wesley's fully developed doctrine is set forth in *A Plain Account of Christian Perfection,* which first appeared in 1766. Its fourth edition, in 1777, remained Wesley's definitive statement of his position. The *Plain Account* contains in full quotation almost everything Wesley had written on the subject before its publication. Here is the doctrine of perfection as he proclaimed and defended it. In reading the *Plain Account,* one must remember that Wesley is delineating in it the *progress* of his thought, and quotations from its earlier sections do not necessarily represent his final position. It is in the latter part of the work that we discover the mature Wesleyan insights into Christian Perfection.

Wesley's own 11-point summary, found in the closing pages of the *Plain Account,* is a succinct presentation of the doctrine:

1. There is such a thing as perfection; for it is again and again mentioned in Scripture.

2. It is not so early as justification; for justified persons are to "go on to perfection" (Heb. vi. 1).

3. It is not so late as death; for St. Paul speaks of living men that were perfect (Phil. iii. 15).

4. It is not absolute. Absolute perfection belongs not to man, nor to angels, but to God alone.

5. It does not make a man infallible: None is infallible, while he remains in the body.

6. Is it sinless? It is not worth while to contend for a term. It is "salvation from sin."

7. It is "perfect love" (1 John iv. 18). This is the essence of it; its properties, or inseparable fruits, are, rejoicing evermore, praying without ceasing, and in everything giving thanks (1 Thess. v. 16 & c).

8. It is improvable. It is so far from lying in an indivisible point, from being incapable of increase, that one perfected in love may grow in grace far swifter than he did before.

9. It is amissible, capable of being lost; of which we have numerous instances. . . .

10. It is constantly both preceded and followed by a gradual work.

11. But is it in itself instantaneous or not? . . . It is often difficult to perceive the instant when a man dies: yet there is

an instant when life ceases. And if ever sin ceases, there must be a last moment of its existence, and a first moment of our deliverance from it.[5]

Such are the salient features of the Wesleyan teaching. But the doctrine has too ancient and continuing a history, as we have seen, to be classified merely as Wesleyan. John Wesley would be the first to repudiate such a suggestion. As Cell observed, he found the truth of perfection "in the warp and woof" of Holy Scripture. His immediate quest was stimulated by reading Thomas a Kempis's *Imitation of Christ,* Bishop Jeremy Taylor's *Rules and Exercises of Holy Living and Dying,* and William Law's *Christian Perfection* and *Serious Call to a Devout and Holy Life.*[6] But long before Wesley and these devotional writers who sparked his desire for holiness, the Greek and Latin Fathers had presented the doctrine in extended exposition, as it has been the purpose of this book to show. In formulating his doctrine of perfection, John Wesley drew from the richest and deepest stream of Christian tradition. The conclusion of Dr. Flew is surely just:

> The doctrine of Christian perfection—understood not as an assertion that a final attainment of the goal of the Christian life is possible in this world, but as a declaration that a supernatural destiny, a relative attainment of the goal which does not exclude growth, is the will of God for us in this world and is attainable—lies not merely upon the bypaths of Christian theology, but upon the high road.[7]

Nevertheless, John Wesley gave the doctrine an entirely new cast. His originality is seen chiefly in the way he put the truth of perfection in the very center of a Protestant understanding of Christian faith. He freed the idea from any notion of merit and presented it as wholly the gift of God's grace. Perfect love is attainable now, by simple faith.

It is because Wesley saw this so clearly that Colin W. Williams questions Cell's claim that Wesley's theology is a "synthesis of the Protestant ethic of grace with the Catholic *ethic* of holiness."[8] In the Catholic ethic merit attaches to holiness, but

---

5. *Ibid.,* 11:441-42.

6. *Ibid.,* 366-67.

7. Flew, *Idea of Perfection,* p. 397.

8. Colin W. Williams, *John Wesley's Theology Today* (London: Epworth Press, 1960), p. 174 (italics added).

Wesley completely removed the doctrine from the order of merit to the order of grace. His view of sanctification is by faith alone. This, says Gordon Rupp, is what gave the Wesleyan gospel its shape and coherence.[9]

In Wesley's view the very center of perfection is *agape*—God's love for man. Its "burning focus" is the Atonement. "Pardoning love is at the root of it all."[10] One of Wesley's most oft quoted verses is the sentence in First John, "We love him, because he first loved us." Love for God is not the natural love of *eros,* but man's answering response to God's prior love. Sanctification for Wesley, like justification, is from first to last the work of God. Justification is what God does *for* us through Christ; sanctification, what He does *in* us by the Holy Spirit. "All things are of God, who has reconciled us to himself by Jesus Christ." This thoroughgoing theocentricity frees his doctrine of perfection from its mystical and humanistic tendencies, which are found in most of the Roman formulations.

Moreover, Wesley has overcome the objectionable features of the Augustinian doctrine of Original Sin. In the *Plain Account* he says, "Adam fell; and his incorruptible body became corruptible; and ever since, it is a clog to the soul, and hinders its operations."[11] But missing is the Platonic idea of an *evil* body and Augustine's emphasis on concupiscence, with its attendant identification of human nature with sinful nature. For Wesley, the meaning of the flesh in Romans 7 is "the whole man *as he is by nature,*"[12] (that is, apart from Christ), embracing both "an inward constraining power of evil inclinations and bodily appetites."[13] The essence of original sin is not lust but "pride, whereby we rob God of his inalienable right, and idolatrously usurp his glory."[14] "The sins of the flesh are the children, not the parents, of pride; and self-love is the root, not the branch, of all evil."[15]

---

9. Cited by Williams, *ibid.,* p. 176.

10. Cell, *Rediscovery of John Wesley,* pp. 297-310.

11. Wesley, *Works,* 11:415.

12. *Explanatory Notes upon the New Testament,* loc. cit., italics added

13. *Ibid.*

14. Wesley, *Works,* 6:60.

15. William R. Cannon, *The Theology of John Wesley* (Nashville: Abingdon-Cokesbury Press, 1946), p. 193.

This Hebraic understanding of sin is Wesley's controlling view as he develops his teaching of sanctification. *If the quintessence of sin is a perverted relationship to God, the quintessence of holiness is a grace-restored right relationship.* For Wesley, therefore, all holiness or perfection is in Christ, and in Christ alone; for only through Him are we restored to fellowship with God. The sin which has spread like a leprosy through the soul of fallen man is healed by the grace which comes through Christ.

> We have this grace, not only from Christ, but in him. For our perfection is not like that of a tree, which flourishes by the sap derived from its own root, but . . . like that of a branch which, united to the vine, bears fruit; but, severed from it, is dried up and withered.[16]

The most eloquent statement of Wesley's view occurs in the latter part of the *Plain Account:*

> The holiest of men still need Christ, as their Prophet, as "the light of the world." For he does not give them light, but from moment to moment; the instant he withdraws all is darkness. They still need Christ as their King; for God does not give them a stock of holiness. But unless they receive a supply every moment, nothing but unholiness would remain. They still need Christ as their Priest, to make atonement for their holy things. Even perfect holiness is acceptable to God only through Jesus Christ.[17]

Williams, therefore, correctly interprets Wesley when he says: "The 'holiness without which no man shall see the Lord,' of which Wesley speaks, is not a holiness that is judged by objective moral standards, but a holiness in terms of unbroken relationship to Christ the Holy One. The perfect Christian is holy, not because he has risen to a required moral standard, but because he lives in this state of unbroken fellowship with Christ."[18]

This is a Protestant doctrine of perfection. Faith *is* perfection. But perfection is not merely imputed, it is also imparted. Through sanctifying faith the believer experiences the infilling of God's love by the gift of the Holy Spirit (cf. Rom. 5:5) and is thereby purified in heart (cf. Acts 15:8-9). "Entire sanctification," Wesley insisted, "is neither more nor less than pure love

---

16. Wesley, *Works*, 11:395.
17. *Ibid.*, 417.
18. Williams, *John Wesley's Theology Today*, p. 175.

—love expelling sin and governing both the heart and life." And this is what he preached: "It is love excluding sin; love filling the heart, taking up the whole capacity of the soul. . . . For as long as love takes up the whole heart, what room is there for sin therein?"[19] In his insistence on this truth Wesley broke with Zinzendorf. *Faith perfected in love through the fullness of the Spirit is the essence of the Wesleyan doctrine of Christian Perfection.*

This doctrine Wesley spoke of as "the grand depositum which God has lodged with the people called Methodist." Philip Schaff calls it Methodism's "last and crowning doctrine." And Frederic Platt identifies it as "pre-eminently the distinctive doctrine" of Methodism.

In his *Understanding the Methodist Church,* Nolan B. Harmon has said:

> The doctrine of Christian perfection has been the one specific doctrinal contribution which Methodism has made to the Church universal. John Wesley called it "the peculiar doctrine committed to our trust." In all else we have been, as we should be, glad and energetic followers in the main stream of Christian belief. But in this one doctrine we stand by ourselves and utter a teaching that reaches up fearlessly and touches the very Scepter of God.[20]

Yet Methodist John L. Peters acknowledges, "In all candor, however, it can scarcely be maintained that in the teaching and preaching of the Church the doctrine holds today, anything like the significant place given it by Wesley."[21] While there are multitudes yet within Methodism who treasure Wesley's doctrine of Christian Perfection, the proclamation of this message has largely passed to denominations of the modern holiness movement. These include The Wesleyan Church, the Free Methodist Church, the Salvation Army, the Church of God (Anderson, Ind.), and the Church of the Nazarene, plus a number of smaller groups including several yearly meetings of the Society of Friends (Quakers). Since the 1860s the interdenominational expression of the Wesleyan doctrine has been the fellowship now known as the Christian Holiness Association. "Its major thrust has always been the promotion of the message

---

19. Wesley, *Works,* 6:46.
20. Cited by Peters, *Christian Perfection and American Methodism,* p. 196.
21. *Ibid.,* pp. 195-96.

of Christian perfection and its practical applications in missions, education, and social concerns."[22]

B. Toward a Theology of Christian Perfection

In the closing pages of this monograph I would like to suggest the outlines of a contemporary doctrine of Christian Perfection. Remembering the path we have taken through the history of Christian thought, several final guidelines seem to be in order.

1. In the first place, a theology of Christian perfection must begin with a lucid definition of sin. Sin can have no meaning apart from the abuse of human freedom. J. S. Whale has said:

> The essence of sin is man's self-centered denial of his distinctive endowment. Its final ground is pride which rebels against God and repudiates his purpose. Its active manifestation is self-love which "changes the glory of the incorruptible God into the image of corruptible man." The freedom of the filial spirit, man's freedom *for* God and *in* God, is perverted to mean freedom *from* God. *Imago Dei* is interpreted to mean "Ye shall be as gods."[23]

If Wesleyan theology is to be biblical, it must repudiate the Augustinian understanding of inbred sin as remaining concupiscence. Moral depravity can be understood only as a consequence of the prior and more basic sin of pride (cf. Rom. 1:18-25). Pride leads man to seek satisfaction in the finite creature rather than in the glorious Creator. "It is in the fixation of man on the finite that the sensual appetites of the lowest kind begin to rise up to claim dominion over him."[24]

Sanctifying grace must heal man at the center of his being; it must crucify his ambitious and pretentious pride. When this is accomplished, the healing grace of God extends to all his affections and desires, making him whole.

2. In the second place, the doctrine of Christian Perfection must avoid the error of making the experience a magical, nonmoral affair. Naturally, a clear formulation of the problem of man's sin will go far in obviating this error. Admittedly, the

---

22. William S. Deal, *The March of Holiness Through the Centuries* (Kansas City: Beacon Hill Press of Kansas City, 1978), p. 91.

23. J. S. Whale, *Christian Doctrine* (New York: The Macmillan Co., 1945), p. 45.

24. Cannon, *Theology of John Wesley,* p. 193.

cleansing which the sanctifying Spirit effects goes deeper than our consciousness. We must always insist, however, that Christian Perfection has its beginning, on the human side, in a *moral crisis* which Wesley called a death to sin, and its continuation in *a maintained relationship* of obedient trust.

The mature Wesley saw this clearly and warned, "Does not talking of a justified or sanctified *state*, tend to mislead men; almost naturally leading them to trust what was done in one moment? Whereas we are every moment pleasing or displeasing to God, according to the whole of our present tempers and outward behavior."[25]

Wesley here guards his position against a charge which some have leveled against him, that he tends to speak of sin as a quantum, a thing like a rotten tooth which must be eradicated. Sin is not a quantity; it is a quality. It is not a substance; it is a condition. Sin is like darkness; it can be expelled only by the light. Wesley also spoke of sin as a disease and of Christ as the Great Physician. Holiness is thus spiritual health restored; but if we are to remain whole we must obey God's laws of moral and spiritual well-being. These are the dynamic terms in which we must think of sin and holiness. Entire sanctification is not a magical act which changes the substance of our souls; it is a moral crisis which restores us to a Christ-centered existence.

The entrance into this life of wholeness and freedom from sin presupposes what Wesley calls "the repentance of believers" —a conviction of remaining sin. The justified believer, through the faithful conviction of the Holy Spirit, becomes painfully aware of his inbred sin—his continuing self-centeredness and double-mindedness. As E. Stanley Jones explains,

> The crisis of conversion brings release from festering sins, and marks the introduction of a new life. Conversion is a glorious release, but not a full release. Festering sins are gone, but the roots of the disease are still there. The new life is introduced, but it is not fully regnant. The old life is subdued, but not surrendered.[26]

The Christian who yearns for personal holiness cannot be satisfied with this double-minded condition. He hungers and

---

25. Minutes of 1770.

26. E. Stanley Jones, *Abundant Living* (New York: Abingdon-Cokesbury Press, 1958), p. 209.

thirsts after righteousness. He must bring the matter to a crisis through a complete surrender of himself to God (see Rom. 6:19). This death to sin moves on a deeper level than the initial surrender to Christ for pardon and new life. Its motivation is a deepened conviction of the pervasive nature of self-idolatry. It is a frank and contrite acknowledgment of one's pettiness, lust, ambition, pride, and selfishness, and a conscious, willing death to self in love to God. We must heed Paul's admonition: "Yield yourselves to God as men who have been brought from death to life, and your members as instruments of righteousness" (Rom. 6:13, RSV).

This death to sin is both gradual and instantaneous, as Wesley says:

> A man may be dying for some time; yet he does not, properly speaking, die, till the instant the soul is separated from the body; and in that instant, he lives the life of eternity. In like manner, he may be dying to sin for some time; yet he is not dead to sin, till sin is separated from his soul; and in that instant, he lives the full life of love. And as the change undergone, when the body dies, is of a different kind, and infinitely greater than any we had known before, yea, such as till then it is impossible to conceive; so the change wrought when the soul dies to sin, is of a different kind, and infinitely greater than any before, and than any can conceive till he experiences it. Yet he still grows in grace, in the knowledge of Christ, in the love and image of God; and will do so, not only till death, but to all eternity.[27]

3. While the repentance of the believer and his death to sin must precede entire sanctification, the one indispensable condition is faith. "But what is the faith whereby we are sanctified —saved from sin, and perfected in love?" Give close attention to Wesley's answer.

> It is a divine evidence and conviction, First, that God hath promised it in the Holy Scripture. Till we are thoroughly satisfied of this, there is no moving one step further. And one would imagine there needed not one word more to satisfy a reasonable man of this, than the ancient promise, "Then will I circumcise thy heart, and the heart of thy seed, to love the Lord thy God with all thy heart, and with all thy soul, and with all thy mind." How clearly does this express the being perfected in love! How strongly imply the being saved

---

27. Wesley, *Works*, 11:402.

from all sin! For as long as love takes up the whole heart, what room is there for sin therein?

It is the divine evidence and conviction, Secondly, that what God hath promised he is able to perform. . . . If God speaks, it shall be done. God said, "Let there be light; and there" is "light!"

It is, Thirdly, a divine evidence and conviction that he is able and willing to do it now. And why not? Is not a moment to him the same as a thousand years? He cannot want more time to accomplish whatever is his will. And he cannot want or stay for any more *worthiness* or *fitness* in the persons he is pleased to honour. We may therefore boldly say, at any point of time, "Now is the day of salvation!" . . .

To this confidence, that God is both able and willing to sanctify us now, there needs to be added one thing more—a divine evidence and conviction that he doeth it. In that hour it is done: God says to the inmost soul, "according to thy faith be it unto thee!" Then the soul is pure from every spot of sin; it is clean "from all unrighteousness." The believer then experiences the deep meaning of those solemn words, "If we walk in the light as he is in the light, we have fellowship one with another, and the blood of Jesus Christ his Son cleanseth us from all sin."[28]

Perfect love is always a gift, to be received any moment by simple faith. In the justified believer God will perform His final work of purification. It is, then, strictly speaking, not an attainment of man, but a boon from God. Believe, and enter in!

4. A scriptural doctrine of Christian Perfection thus declares that entire sanctification is the action of God, who by the Holy Spirit frees the soul from sin and inaugurates a new pattern of inward devotement.

It is the ministry of God the Holy Spirit to "enter into the recesses of the human spirit and to work from within the subjectivity of man." From within our human being the Spirit vitalizes, sanctifies, and strengthens. The work of the Spirit by which we are made whole is happening "because the grace of God is not only something without us, manifest in the death and passion of Jesus Christ, but is a power at work within us, directing its impact at the very citadel of our wills. This inward grace is God personally at work within us. It is God the Holy Ghost."[29]

---

28. *Ibid.*, 6:52-53.

29. C. W. Lowry, *The Trinity and Christian Devotion* (New York: Harper and Bros., 1946), p. 74.

Dr. Cell remarks pertinently: "Holiness is the third term of the Trinitarian revelation of God. This is the highest conceivable position for the doctrine of holiness in the Christian faith and its interpretation." He then quotes Wesley's comment: "The title Holy applied to the Spirit of God not only denotes that he is holy in his own nature, but that he makes us so; that he is the great fountain of holiness to his church. The Holy Spirit is the principle of the conversion and entire sanctification of our hearts and lives."[30]

Reason, Scripture, and experience make us bold to assert, therefore, that when the believer confesses his remaining sin, yields up his heart in loving surrender, and trusts God's promises, the Holy Spirit possesses and cleanses the inner sanctuary of his soul and floods his being with the love of God.

> Q. But how do you know that you are sanctified, saved from your inward corruption?
>
> A. I can know it no otherwise than I know I am justified. *Hereby know we that we are of God* in either sense *by the Spirit that He hath given us.* We know it by the witness and by the fruit of the Spirit. And, first, by the witness. As, when we were justified, the Spirit bore witness with our spirit, that our sins were forgiven; so, when we are sanctified, He bore witness that they were taken away.[31]

This is the full assurance of faith. Lycurgus Starkey comments: "Inwardly to *know* the temple has been cleansed by God, who remains in the fullness of His Spirit as its consecration is the significance and content of this full assurance."[32]

5. A final feature of a theology of perfection is a frank recognition of its relative nature. It is evangelical perfection. In place of the Mosaic law God has established another law through Christ, namely the law of faith. As Wesley reminds us, "Not every one that *doeth,* but every one that *believeth,* now receiveth righteousness . . . that is, he is justified, sanctified, and glorified."

> Is love the fulfilling of this law?
> Unquestionably it is. The whole law under which we now

---

30. Cited by Cell, *Rediscovery of John Wesley,* p. 353.

31. Wesley, *Works,* 11:420.

32. Lycurgus Starkey, *The Work of the Holy Spirit* (New York: Abingdon Press, 1962), p. 67.

live is fulfilled by love (Rom. 13:9-10). Faith working or animated by love is all that God now requires of man.

How is love "the end of the commandment"?

It is the point aimed at by the whole and every part of the Christian institution. The foundation is faith, purifying the heart; and the end love, preserving a good conscience.

What love is this?

The loving the Lord our God with all our heart, mind, soul, and strength; and the loving of neighbour, every man as ourselves, as our own souls.[33]

W. E. Sangster thinks that "perfect love" is the true name for Wesley's doctrine.[34] This name underscores the positive, social nature of holiness. Wesley himself shrank from using the term "sinless perfection,"[35] since the saintliest of Christians "come short of the law of love" as it is set forth in the thirteenth chapter of First Corinthians.[36] Because of their ignorance, those who have been perfected in love are guilty of what Wesley calls "involuntary transgressions"[37] of God's law. "It follows that the most perfect have continual need of the merits of Christ, even for their actual transgressions, and may say for themselves, as well as for their brethren, 'Forgive us our trespasses.'"[38] Moreover, "none feel their need of Christ like these; none so entirely depend upon him. For Christ does not give life to the soul separate from him, but in and with, himself." He then quotes the words of Jesus, "Without [or separate from] me ye can do nothing."[39]

Wesley thus makes two qualifying points. First, Christian Perfection is not absolute but relative to our understanding of God's will. Hence the fully sanctified man feels deeply his imperfections and lapses from the perfect law of love and maintains a penitent and open spirit which saves him from Pharisaism. He never forgets that he is justified, not by works, but by grace, and thus leans wholly upon the Lord. Secondly, he knows that the perfect love which is God's gift to him through the Spirit is "moment by moment" impartation of Christ to his soul. With Paul such a person confesses: "I know that in me (that is, in my flesh [myself apart from Christ's indwelling

33. Wesley, *Works*, 11:414-15.

34. W. E. Sangster, *The Path to Perfection* (New York: Abingdon Press, 1944), pp. 142-49.

35. Wesley, *Works*, 11:418.

36. *Ibid.*, 417.   37. *Ibid.*, 396.   38. *Ibid.*, 394-95.   39. *Ibid.*, 395.

presence|), dwelleth no good thing" (Rom. 7:18). There is no room for boasting save in the grace of Christ, who pours God's *agape* into my being.

The scriptural basis for this view of "imperfect perfection" is found in Phil. 3:11-15 and Rom. 8:17-27. Though by the grace of God we may have been brought into spiritual adulthood (love made perfect), we are still, in the words of E. Stanley Jones, "Christians in the making." We have not yet attained to the mark of final Christlikeness for which we were claimed of God through the gospel; but we do have a singleness of purpose which permits the Spirit to carry us toward that goal with steadiness (cf. Heb. 6:1).

In Romans we are reminded that our Christian existence in the Spirit is an existence in the "time between the times," that is, in "this present time" between Pentecost and the Parousia. By the grace of God we may be no longer "in the flesh but in the Spirit, if the Spirit of God really dwells in" us (Rom. 8:9, RSV). But we are still in a body which is not redeemed and we must suffer the "infirmities of the flesh"—the racial effects of sin in our bodies and minds, the scars from past sinful living, our prejudices which hinder God's purposes, our neuroses which bring emotional depressions and cause us at times to act "out of character," our temperamental idiosyncrasies, our human weariness and fretfulness, and a thousand faults our mortal flesh is heir to. "For we have this treasure in earthen vessels, that the excellency of the power may be of God, and not of us" (2 Cor. 4:7).

A full-orbed doctrine of Christian Perfection must place the truth of holiness within the framework of "this present age," which is characterized by these "infirmities of the flesh." Thus Paul declares that we have been "saved in hope" (Rom. 8:25)— the hope of that final stroke of sovereign grace which shall bring to consummation that grand work of sanctification which began when we were converted. This is the hope of the resurrection. Wesley would agree with Karl Barth, who comments on this Romans text, "If Christianity be not altogether restless eschatology, there remains in it no relationship to Christ."[40] Ours is indeed a "theology of hope."

---

40. Karl Barth, *The Epistle to the Romans,* trans. Edwyn Hoskins (London: Oxford University Press, 1933), p. 314.

Some people scorn such a doctrine of "imperfect perfection." But to deny the possibility of being sanctified by the Spirit and knowing God's perfect love because we are still finite creatures subject to the limitations of an earthly existence, is to miss something which is vital to New Testament Christianity. We therefore subscribe to "the Wesleyan paradox" of Christian Perfection. The full truth is not gained by removing the tension between the two poles ("perfect"—"not yet perfected") but by holding these two truths with equal emphasis. Only thus does the Christian life flower into Christlikeness.

We devoutly believe that God has entrusted to those of us who call ourselves Wesleyan "the grand depositum" of this New Testament teaching of heart holiness. If we cease to "groan after" and "seek" this perfection in Christ, if we fail to make this emphasis the focus of salvation truth in our preaching and teaching, if we do not in brokenness and openness appropriate the full blessing of Pentecost in individual life and in the life of the church, we will forfeit our birthright as the followers of John Wesley. Most tragic of all, we will fail God, who has commissioned us to "spread scriptural holiness" to the ends of the earth.

Bibliography

Aulén, Gustaf. *Christus Victor.* Translated by A. G. Herbert. New York: The Macmillan Company, 1945.

————. *The Faith of the Christian Church.* Translated by Eric H. Wahlstrom. Philadelphia: Fortress Press, 1960.

Barth, Karl. *The Epistle to the Romans.* Translated by Edwyn Hoskins. London: Oxford University Press, 1933.

Bettenson, Henry, ed. and trans. *The Early Christian Fathers: A Selection from the Writings of the Fathers from St. Clement of Rome to St. Athanasius.* London: Oxford University Press, 1956.

Bowman, John Wick. *Prophetic Realism and the Gospel.* Philadelphia: Westminster Press, 1955.

Brunner, Emil. *The Christian Doctrine of God.* Translated by Olive Wyon. London: Lutterworth Press, 1960.

Callihan, Virginia. *St. Gregory of Nyssa, Ascetical Works.* Washington, D.C.: The Catholic University Press, 1967.

Cannon, William R. *The Theology of John Wesley.* Nashville: Abingdon-Cokesbury Press, 1946.

Cell, George Croft. *The Rediscovery of John Wesley.* New York: Henry Holt and Co., 1935.

Deal, William S. *The March of Holiness Through the Centuries.* Kansas City: Beacon Hill Press of Kansas City, 1978.

Edersheim, Alfred. *Bible History: Old Testament.* Grand Rapids: William B. Eerdmans Publishing Company, 1949.

Eichrodt, Walther. *Theology of the Old Testament.* Translated by J. A. Walker. Philadelphia: Westminster Press, 1961.

Flew, R. Newton. *The Idea of Perfection.* London: Oxford University Press, 1934.

Girgensohn, Herbert. *Teaching Luther's Catechism.* Translated by John W. Doberstein. Philadelphia: Muhlenberg Press, 1959. (In chapter 8 this was quoted in a book by Donald Metz entitled, *Studies in Biblical Holiness.*)

Jacob, Edmond. *Theology of the Old Testament.* Translated by Arthur W. Heathcoat and Philip J. Allcock. New York: Harper and Brothers, 1958.

Jones, E. Stanley. *Abundant Living.* New York: Abingdon-Cokesbury Press, 1958.

Knight, John A. *The Holiness Pilgrimage.* Kansas City: Beacon Hill Press of Kansas City, 1973.

Kuyper, Abraham. *The Work of the Holy Spirit.* Translated by Henri DeVries. New York: Funk and Wagnalls, 1900.

Lightfoot, J. B. *The Apostolic Fathers.* Grand Rapids: Baker Book House, 1956.

Lowry, C. W. *The Trinity and Christian Devotion.* New York: Harper and Brothers, 1946.

Lueker, E. L., Editor. *Lutheran Cyclopedia.* St. Louis: Concordia Publishing House, 1954.

Luther, Martin. *Works of Martin Luther.* Philadelphia: Westminster Press, 1932.

McGiffert, A. C. *A History of Christian Thought.* New York: Charles Scribner's Sons, 1949.

Metz, Donald. *Studies in Biblical Holiness.* Kansas City: Beacon Hill Press of Kansas City, 1971.

Miller, Howard V. *When He Is Come.* Kansas City: Beacon Hill Press, 1941.

Mondesert, C. *Clement d'Alexandrie.* Paris: 1944.

Morris, Leon. *The Epistles of Paul to the Thessalonians.* Grand Rapids; William B. Eerdmans Publishing Co., 1957.

Otto, Rudolph. *The Idea of the Holy.* Translated by John W. Harvey. London: Oxford University Press, 1924.

Outler, Albert. *John Wesley.* New York: Oxford University Press, 1964.

Peters, John L. *Christian Perfection and American Methodism.* New York and Nashville: Abingdon Press, 1946.

Pope, William Burton. *A Compendium of Christian Theology.* London: Published for the Wesleyan Conference Office, 1880.

Robinson, J. A. T. *The Body, a Study in Pauline Theology.* London: SCM Press, 1966.

Sangster, W. E. *The Path to Perfection.* New York: Abingdon-Cokesbury Press, 1944.

Schechter, Solomon. *Some Aspects of Rabbinic Theology.* New York: The Macmillan Company, 1910.

Smith, C. Ryder. *The Bible Doctrine of Man.* London: The Epworth Press, 1951.

Snaith, Norman H. *The Distinctive Ideas of the Old Testament.* London: The Epworth Press, 1960.

Starkey, Lycurgus. *The Work of the Holy Spirit.* New York: Abingdon-Cokesbury Press, 1962.

Tillich, Paul. *A History of Christian Thought.* Edited by Carl Braaten. New York and Evanston: Harper and Row, 1968.

Turner, George Allen. *The More Excellent Way.* Winona Lake, Ind.: Light and Life Press, 1952.

———. *The Vision Which Transforms.* Kansas City: Beacon Hill Press, 1964.

Walker, Williston. *A History of the Christian Church.* New York: Charles Scribner's Sons, 1944.

Wesley, John. *A Christian Library.* London: T. Cordeus, 1819.

———. *Explanatory Notes upon the New Testament.* London: The Epworth Press, 1950.

———. *Works.* Kansas City: Nazarene Publishing House.

Whale, J. S. *Christian Doctrine.* New York: McMillan Co., 1945.

Wiley, H. Orton. *Christian Theology.* Kansas City: Beacon Hill Press, 1945.

Williams, Colin W. *John Wesley's Theology Today.* London: Epworth Press, 1960.

Walvoord, John F. *Doctrine of the Holy Spirit.* Findlay, Ohio: Dunham Publishing Company, 1958.

Wood, Simon P. *Christ the Educator.* Fathers of the Church, Inc., 1954.

Historical Sources

Against Heresies, III

Aquinas, Thomas. *Summa Theologica*

———. *De Perfectione*

A Testimony to the Truth of God.

Athanasius. *Vit. Ant.*

Augustine. *Retractions.*

———. *De natura et gratia.*

———. *Epistolae.*

———. *De spir. et lit.*

———. *De Trinita.*

———. *De Mor. eccl. cath.*

———. *De civ. Dei.*

———. *De serm. Dom. in monte.*

Basil. *Reg. fus. tract.*

———. *Reg. brev. tract.*

Clement. *Paedagogus.*

———. *Protrepticus.*

———. *Stromateis.*

———. *Quis Dives Salvetur.*

Encyclopedia of Religion and Ethics, ed. James Hastings. New York: Charles Scribner's Sons, 1928.

Fox, George. *Journal.*

Francois de Sales. *Introduction to the Devout Life*

―――. *Treatise on the Love of God.*

―――. *Oeuvres.*

Francois Fenelon. *Christian Perfection.* Charles F. Whiston, ed. Translated by Mildred Whitney Stillman. New York and London: Harper and Brothers publishers, 1947.

Hermann. *Communion with God.* English translation.

History of Dogma, vii.

In Cant. S. Bernard of Clairvaux (A commentary on the Song of Songs)

Inge. *Christian Mysticism* (quoted by Flew).

Institutes of the Christian Religion, by John Calvin, translated by John Allen. Philadelphia: Board of Christian Education. Vol. I

Luther, Martin. *Werke.* Erlangen ed., xxv.

―――. *Table-Talk.* No. CCLVI

Origen. *Contra Celsus.*

―――. *De principiis.*

The Assembly's Shorter Catechism. Perth, Scotland: 1765.

Werner. *Duns Scotus.* 2 (quoted by Flew).